PREPARED

FISHING

Henry Gilbey

FISHING

Henry Gilbey

DK

LONDON, NEW YORK, MUNICH, MELBOURNE, DELHI

Project Editor	Steve Setford
Art Editor	Peter Radcliffe
Project Manager	Nigel Duffield
Editorial Lead	Heather Jones

This is an abridged and revised edition of *Eyewitness Companion*
produced for Dorling Kindersley by
Schermuly Design Co.

First American Edition, 2008

Published in the United States by
DK Publishing, Inc.
375 Hudson Street,
New York, New York 10014

07 08 09 10 11 10 9 8 7 6 5 4 3 2 1

For more information on the Boy Scouts of America programs,
visit www.scouting.org

A Cataloging-in-Publication record for this book is
available from the Library of Congress.

ISBN 978-0-7566-3724-8

DK books are available at special discounts for bulk
purchases for sales promotions, premiums, fund-raising, or
educational use. For details, contact: DK Publishing Special
Markets, 375 Hudson Street, New York, NY 10014 or
SpecialSales@dk.com

Color reproduction by GRB Editrice, Italy
Printed and bound in China by L. Rex Printing Co. Ltd.

IMPORTANT NOTICE
Do not practice any techniques described in this book
on private land or in private waters without the owner's
permission, and obey all laws relating to the protection of
land, property, plants, and animals.

Discover more at
www.dk.com

CONTENTS

BOY SCOUTS OF AMERICA

The mission of the Boy Scouts of America is to prepare young people to make ethical and moral choices over their lifetimes by instilling in them the values of the Scout Oath and Law. The programs of the Boy Scouts of America—Cub Scouting, Boy Scouting, Varsity Scouting, and Venturing—pursue these aims through methods designed for the age and maturity of the participants.

Cub Scouting: A family- and home-centered program for boys in the first through fifth grade (or 7, 8, 9 and 10 years old). Cub Scouting's emphasis is on quality programs at the local level, where the most boys and families are involved. Fourth and fifth grade (or 10-year-old) boys are called Webelos (WE'll BE LOyal Scouts) and participate in more advanced activities that begin to prepare them to become Boy Scouts.

Boy Scouting: A program for boys 11 through 17 designed to achieve the aims of Scouting through a vigorous outdoor program and peer group leadership with the counsel of an adult Scoutmaster. Boys may also become Boy Scouts if they have earned the Arrow of Light Award or have completed the fifth grade.

Varsity Scouting: An active, exciting program for young men 14 through 17 built around five program fields of emphasis: advancement, high adventure, personal development, service, and special programs and events.

Venturing: This is for young men and women ages 14 through 20. It includes challenging high-adventure activities, sports, and hobbies for teenagers that teach leadership skills, provide opportunities to teach others, and to learn and grow in a supporting, caring, and fun environment.

For more on Scouting programs visit www.scouting.org

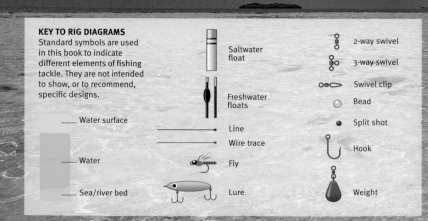

KEY TO RIG DIAGRAMS
Standard symbols are used in this book to indicate different elements of fishing tackle. They are not intended to show, or to recommend, specific designs.

Water surface

Water

Sea/river bed

Saltwater float

Freshwater floats

Line

Wire trace

Fly

Lure

2-way swivel

3-way swivel

Swivel clip

Bead

Split shot

Hook

Weight

Introduction

FISHING IS ABOUT TRYING TO OUTWIT nature, and since our natural world is delightfully unpredictable, we, as anglers, are dealing with variables we simply cannot control. This book is full of useful information and is an excellent guide to get you started, but you will soon learn to think for yourself and to try different things. While the fishing strategies in this book will give you every chance of success, always remember that there is nothing truly definite about the methods you can use in any scenario.

A key attribute of a naturally gifted angler is to strive to discover more and more information in the pursuit of the fish. Take a strategy and advance it to suit you, and then share what you've discovered with others. Most anglers are extremely socially interactive, and information is continually passed around and then further adapted. This information

exchange means that fishing is a sport that is always growing and evolving.

Fishing is full of surprises. Most anglers, at some point in their fishing, make the mistake of thinking that they have "gotten one over on" the fish, but nature always likes to give a little kick to remind us that we are but humans. Fishing gives you the chance to learn something new every single time you practice it. If fishing becomes your lifelong hobby, you will find that you never stop learning.

Above all, this book will introduce you to a sport that is tremendous fun. Put simply, anglers go fishing because they enjoy it. As you progress and become more proficient, hold on to the memory of the first fish you ever caught, and recall your beaming smile and shrieks of joy. Fishing offers a lifetime of simple fun; if this book goes any way toward helping you achieve that, then it will have done its job.

Getting started

Before you take to the water, spend some time learning about the rules and regulations associated with angling. Learn where to find up-to-date information, and where to meet fellow anglers. Above all, spend time around water to pick up valuable advice from other anglers, which will help make your fishing experiences both pleasurable and safe. The more background knowledge you can acquire, the more kinds of fishing you can try.

Fishing for the first time

Fishing is essentially a very simple activity. In its most basic form, it comprises no more than the attempt to fool a fish into taking a bait or artificial lure. Newcomers to the sport should not be daunted by the special terminology or the vast array of tackle choices available.

GETTING HOOKED

An angler never forgets his or her first catch, whether it be a mackerel caught from a vacation pier or a largemouth bass in a warm Florida lake. Many novice anglers are lucky enough to catch a fish on their first fishing trip and become "hooked" for life. The experience of outwitting both the wild animal and the environment that it inhabits lends an insight into what life might have been like for our prehistoric hunter-gatherer ancestors. Many of today's anglers will never eat the fish they catch, but the fact remains that humans first learned to fish in order to obtain food.

Going fishing for the first time is all about having fun. Although fishing is a serious sport, for many—especially to newcomers to the activity—it is, above all, a pastime or a hobby to be enjoyed.

PASSING ON KNOWLEDGE

The best way to learn to fish is to go out with an experienced angler, whether a professional teacher or guide, or a willing friend or relative. One of the aspects of the sport of fishing that makes it so special is the fact that many experienced anglers are happy to impart their hard-earned knowledge to enthusiastic novices. Fishing as a sport is constantly evolving and this happens because each generation of anglers fish in their own way, and then pass on their experience and knowledge to the next generation. However, the benefits of sharing fishing know-how are not all one-way. The sheer

FISHING WITH CHILDREN
If there are young children in your group, make sure that they are aware of basic water safety rules and how to handle equipment properly. However, you also need to make the experience fun for them.

thrill of fishing and catching fish, which suddenly begins to seize the first-timer, can be infectious. In this way, bringing a newcomer into the sport can often rekindle a dormant love for the activity in someone who has perhaps not been fishing for years. Nobody is ever going to care whether that first fish is a monster or a minnow, but nothing grabs the interest to the same degree as actually catching a fish.

FISHING SAFETY

Fishing is about trying to outwit nature, and in so doing it requires proximity to perhaps the most unpredictable element: water. One of the first lessons the fishing novice must learn is to place safety above all else when planning a fishing trip—for example, by taking into account weather forecasts, or by wearing a buoyancy aid when on a boat. Shore-fishing, especially

YOUR FIRST FISH
Few ever forget the thrill of their first catch, however modest its size. And even after years of fishing, an echo of that excitement is relived after every catch.

LEARNING WITH AN EXPERT
Nothing beats professional instruction, especially for fly-fishing, where casting is vital. All over the world you will find qualified instructors and guides.

from rocks in tidal or potentially rough waters, requires constant vigilance for changes in the condition of the sea. In addition, one of the most vital safety precautions is not to fish near overhead power lines with long rods and not to fish when lightning is forecast. This is because modern fishing rods make excellent conductors of electricity.

Fishing clubs and tackle shops

There are plenty of ways to meet fellow anglers, whether your aim is to get instruction, swap ideas, or simply access new waters. Fishing by its very nature is often a solitary pastime, but clubs, tackle shops, and Internet forums provide the opportunity for anglers to get together.

LOCAL CLUBS

In most areas you can find a thriving fishing club. Ask in your local tackle shop, look in the local press, and search on the Internet for a fishing club that suits the kind of fishing you want to do. Most clubs have regular meetings, fishing days, and possibly even instructional sessions for beginners. Many also have access to stretches of waters that otherwise would not be available and/or for which the charges are far lower than to nonmembers. Clubs often run competitions that can attract large numbers of anglers, and these might give you a taste of competitive fishing. Some clubs also organize fishing trips to waters farther afield, and even to different countries. But most of all, a fishing club provides a social center for the angler to spend time with other anglers and take part in the age-old traditions of talking, sharing fishing knowledge and, of course, telling the tale of "the one that got away."

TACKLE SHOPS

Your local tackle shop is usually the busy hub of the local fishing scene. While there is a thriving network of discounted mail order Internet shops, local shops can often give advice about baits and tackle that work in the area. Many people who work in tackle shops are

FISHING WITH FRIENDS
Nothing beats a fishing expedition with a group of friends. Sharing the experience with those who love fishing as much as you is what the sport is all about.

GETTING ADVICE
A good local fishing-tackle shop will be able to offer plenty of up-to-date, reliable local fishing advice that is invaluable to the visiting or novice angler.

themselves avid and skillful anglers. Local tackle shops are often like a kind of club where people stop to talk and swap information. Whenever you go fishing away from home, anywhere in the world, be sure to take the opportunity to drop into the nearest tackle shop and spend time talking to the people there.

SPECIALIST FISHING INSTRUCTORS

There are plenty of fly-fishing instructors who are qualified to teach about fly-casting and the techniques involved in this discipline. You can find them by searching on the Internet or by asking in tackle shops. Many instructors also provide guiding services on local waters. Boat-fishing skippers and guides, especially in sea fishing, will always provide as much good advice as you are willing to ask for. The sensible traveling angler will always seek advice from their guide. There are plenty of fishing magazines that cover all the basic and more advanced skills, and these are useful resources. However, nothing beats actually getting out on the water and learning by trial and error. An instructor and teacher is there to help put you on the right path and teach you the fundamental skills that will allow you to progress in your own time.

FISHING WEBSITES AND FORUMS

Increasingly the world of fishing is online, whether through web-based magazines and tackle shops, or in international forums. Even forums that deal with local fishing often attract foreign anglers seeking to learn other tactics, and this works both ways. These can be fantastic places to share ideas, talk about local fishing conditions, plan overseas fishing trips and, of course, post catch shots from your latest trip.

Fishing licenses

While many waters are free to all for fishing, in many places an angler will require some kind of fishing license or permit. It is essential to check up in advance on the regulations that apply to the waters—whether freshwater or saltwater—that you intend to fish.

LICENSES, PERMITS, AND TICKETS

In many countries, the angler is required to hold a license or permit that covers fishing, whether in freshwater or in the sea. Such regulations are usually administered by a governmental organization. The angler may have to buy an additional license that permits fishing for migratory species (usually salmon). Many lakes and rivers can be fished only by purchasing a ticket for the period in which you intend to fish; while others are available only to their owners or to club members. Be sure to find out (in local tackle shops or on the Internet) whether you must seek local permission or otherwise pay to fish the water.

BUYING YOUR LICENSE
Many fishing lodges can obtain a license or permit for you if you ask. Carry it at all times when you are fishing; you might be asked to show it.

FRESHWATER LICENSES

Most freshwater fishing requires that the angler purchases a license. Much of this money goes into restocking and water-management programs. A different license may be needed for fishing for game species, especially if you are targeting salmon. Be careful to check whether you may take fish home; fines for infringement are often very severe. Be aware that there are closeseasons for some species, often timed to protect breeding times. In addition, local, temporary closures can be imposed. Some regulations also govern fishing methods. Ask about local rules, such as those regarding the fishing methods permitted, the use of barbless hooks, if keep nets can be used, or whether or not you can groundbait.

SALTWATER LICENSES

Sea fishing in much of the world is free, but some countries require you to purchase a sea-fishing license. Be sure to check before going fishing; ignorance of the local regulations is unlikely to impress the fishing authorities. Licenses and permits are usually purchased in local tackle shops or online. Many species are closely protected and you will be allowed to take only a limited number of these to eat.

FREEDOM OF THE SEA
Throughout much of the world you may fish the oceans for free. Always check for no-go zones and take limits for the fish you are targeting.

EXCLUSIVE RIVER FISHING
The licensing rules for general freshwater fishing and fly-fishing often differ. Many fly-only rivers are tightly controlled and access may be limited.

Fishing tackle

There are many different items of fishing
tackle, from a variety of rods for different
types of fishing, through to intricate,
high-tech gadgets—such as electronic bite
alarms—that will increase your success.
Learning about essential tackle items will
enable you to equip yourself correctly
to catch any number of fish species in
a range of ways. Just wearing the right
clothing can be the key to making fishing
more comfortable, and more effective.

Rod basics

Fishing rods are available in a wide variety of lengths, weights, uses, actions, and even colors. There are core "families" of rods that correspond to each of the main categories of fishing. Anglers choose a rod to suit the type of fishing they plan to undertake.

ROD CHOICES

In its most basic form, a fishing rod is designed to cast or drop the lure, fly, or bait out to the fish and then act as a support to the line when playing the hooked fish. But there are huge differences in how rods are designed to achieve these functions, both in their construction and in what the individual angler wants from their rod. Rod preferences are personal and there will always be debate as to the merits of different actions, looks, prices, and feel. There are no rules with fishing rods, but when making your choice, get advice from an expert who knows your needs.

UNDER PRESSURE

A rod acts as a shock absorber to protect the line and keep the hook in place as fish fight. An angler soon learns how much pressure to apply.

ROD ACTION

The action of a rod refers to how much of the rod bends when it is put under pressure, whether during casting or when you are trying to land a fish. A rod with a fast action bends mainly in the top third of the rod, a medium- (or moderate-) action rod bends in the top half of the rod, and a slow- (or through-) action rod bends from the lower third of the rod through to the tip. Rods with more "forgiving" medium or slow actions are well-suited to beginners because they are easier to cast.

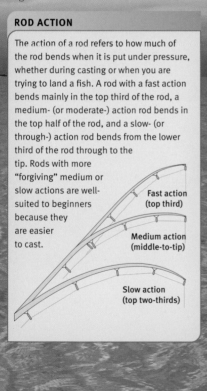

Fast action
(top third)

Medium action
(middle-to-tip)

Slow action
(top two-thirds)

ROD LENGTHS

The length of a rod affects its performance: a long rod will cast farther than a shorter one for the same effort. However, a longer rod can be impractical. Rod length may also be a matter of national preference; for example, US anglers tend to favor spinning rods that are short with a fast action, but in the UK a longer rod with a slower action is usually preferred.

SHORT ROD
Often used on a boat, a short rod provides the huge lifting power needed to fight very large fish.

LONG ROD
A long rod allows you to cast long distances from the shore, but can be heavy to hold.

PARTS OF A ROD

All fishing rods share the same basic components. A rod "blank" is simply the bare rod, without any hardware attached. Many anglers buy blanks and build their own rods. Spinning and fly reels (*see* pp. 24–25) require a rod with the rings on the underside of the blank, whereas conventional reels are designed to be used with the rings on the top.

SECURING RING FOR HOOK
A small ring at the base of the rod blank near the front grip provides a safe securing point for the hook when the rod is rigged but not in use.

REEL SEAT
The fixture that secures the reel to the rod is usually fixed in place, but some reel seats are adjustable.

END CAP
The bottom end of the rod is protected from damage by the end cap.

Front (or fore-) grip

Rod blank

Handle

Intermediate rings

TIP RING
The ring (also known as an eye or guide) on the tip of the rod takes the most strain and needs to be checked regularly for wear. A damaged ring can shred the line.

FIRST RING
The first ring is the largest ring. It helps to control the line as it peels off the reel during a cast.

FERRULE
Also known as spigots, ferrules are used to connect the sections of a fishing rod. Some rods are in one piece, but others are multi-sectioned. The areas around joints are usually strengthened.

Types of rods

Each type of rod is designed to enable the angler to cope with the demands of its intended use. For example, a float rod is typically delicate and sensitive, while a boat rod is short and robust to provide the lifting power required for fishing in deep water.

THE RIGHT ROD FOR THE JOB

Most rods can be used for many different kinds of fishing. But the lighter, more delicate specialty designs, such as float rods, are best used for their intended purposes. Although many rods can be used for both freshwater and saltwater fishing, rods intended primarily for freshwater fishing are not built to withstand the corrosive action of salt.

FLOAT RODS

Although often used to target fish of a modest size, float rods have a relatively slow action and are strong enough to comfortably land big fish.

13–15-FT (4–4.6-M) FLOAT ROD

Long float rods are very sensitive, allowing the angler to cast light floats. This model comes with an optional extra section, should greater length be required.

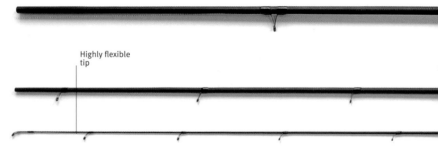

Highly flexible tip

SPINNING AND CASTING RODS

Spinning and casting rods are designed to cast a variety of artificial lures. The term "spinning" refers to fishing with all kinds of artificial lures, both hard and soft. Look for a rod with an action that gives the flexibility you prefer.

9-FT (2.7-M) SPINNING ROD

Used in freshwater and saltwater, this rod is rated to cast terminal tackle that weighs ½–1½ oz (15–45 g).

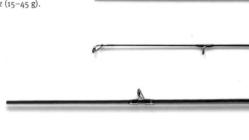

7-FT (2.1-M) CASTING ROD

Ideal for catching bass and pike, this rod is designed to be used with a conventional reel (see pp.24–27).

ROD RESTS AND BITE ALARMS

Many freshwater fishing methods require the rod to have a support system such as a rest or stand. Modern-day carp fishing, in particular, has become highly technical. Rods and reels are often set up on "pod" systems that hold everything steady and accessible. These pods may also incorporate bite alarms that alert you to a potential bite when you are not holding the rod (*right*).

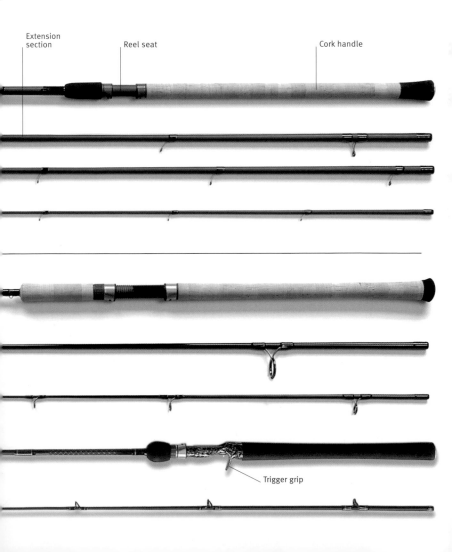

Extension section

Reel seat

Cork handle

Trigger grip

BOAT RODS

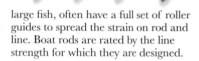

Rods used on boats are shorter than other types. This gives increased lifting power for fishing beneath the boat, and a shorter rod is easier to use in a restricted space. Powerful boat rods, for catching large fish, often have a full set of roller guides to spread the strain on rod and line. Boat rods are rated by the line strength for which they are designed.

SURFCASTING RODS

Most surfcasting rods are long in order to help the angler to cast a long way, which is often necessary when fishing from the shore. Softer tipped rods are easier to cast and protect soft baits from damage during casting. Rock-fishing rods are special surfcasting rods that are specifically designed for fishing for hard-fighting quarry over rough ground.

FRESHWATER FLY-FISHING RODS

Rod requirements for fly-fishing range from fishing with the tiniest flies on a small stream, through to fishing for salmon on large, fast-flowing rivers. Fly rods, lines, and reels are rated according to the AFTM code—for example, a #8 (8-weight) fly rod is rated to cast a #8 line.

10-FT (3-M) #5 RIVER AND LAKE FLY ROD
This general-purpose, four-piece fly rod is easy to carry. It will cope well with a wide variety of freshwater fly-fishing situations.

DOUBLE-HANDED SALMON ROD
This 14-ft (4.3-m) #9 fly rod, built to facilitate double-handed casting techniques, will cope with big rivers and tricky conditions, but remains light and responsive.

SALTWATER FLY-FISHING RODS

Virtually all modern saltwater fly rods divide into at least four sections, making them easy to transport in bags. High-tech materials mean that these rods are immensely strong and can withstand the most extreme saltwater fly-fishing. For the more advanced fly-angler there are rods with a faster, stiffer action that produce faster line speeds and thus longer casts—a faster line also cuts through the wind and can give better fly presentation when this is needed. Rods with a more forgiving, slow action are better for beginners. Some heavier class fly rods have an extra grip above the foregrip for fighting big fish.

9-FT (2.7-M) #12 SALTWATER FLY ROD
This powerful fly rod is able to cope with heavy lines, large flies, and big fish. It may be harder to cast, but its greater strength is necessary for more extreme fly-fishing.

Ultra-slim rod blank to minimize wind resistance

9-FT (2.7-M) #8 SALTWATER FLY ROD
A good all-arounder, this precision-casting saltwater fly rod is suitable for a variety of applications, including catching bonefish on the flats.

Fast-action tip

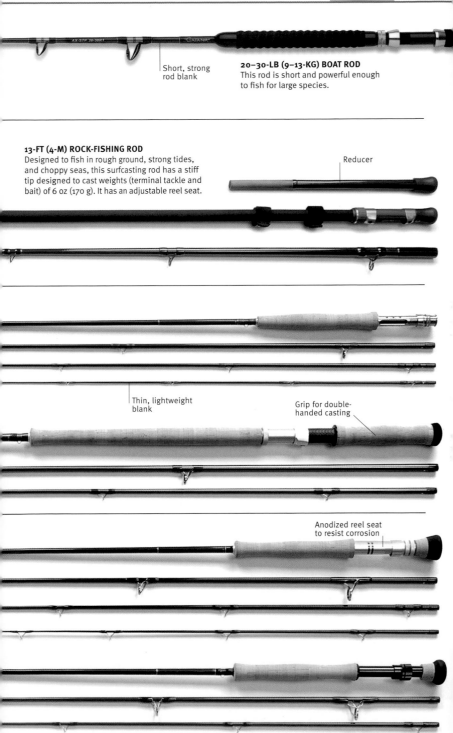

Short, strong
rod blank

20–30-LB (9–13-KG) BOAT ROD
This rod is short and powerful enough
to fish for large species.

13-FT (4-M) ROCK-FISHING ROD
Designed to fish in rough ground, strong tides,
and choppy seas, this surfcasting rod has a stiff
tip designed to cast weights (terminal tackle and
bait) of 6 oz (170 g). It has an adjustable reel seat.

Reducer

Thin, lightweight
blank

Grip for double-
handed casting

Anodized reel seat
to resist corrosion

Reel basics

The primary function of a reel is to store line and enable the angler to cast it out to the fish and then retrieve it. Its secondary function is to help the angler to tire the hooked fish, by means of a drag system that can be adjusted to set the line tension as required.

REEL CATEGORIES

There are three main types of reels: spinning, conventional, and fly. Fly and conventional reels have a revolving spool, turning the handle of which winches in the line. Spinning reels have a spool that stays stationary, and turning the handle causes line to be wrapped via a rotating arm, called the bale arm. The spool of a conventional reel revolves several times for each turn of the handle, which helps you to reel in line quickly. Most modern reels have a drag or clutch system, to allow hooked fish to take the line at a tension set by the angler.

PLAYING A FISH ON A FLY REEL
When fish want to run, the reel allows them to take line against the amount of tension provided by the drag system. This makes fish work for the line they take.

ATTACHING A FLY REEL

The simplest way to attach a fly reel to the rod is from the top, because it is easier to see what you are doing, although in fact fly reels are used below the rod (see above). When the reel is in use, be sure to check regularly that the reel seat and locking rings are tight.

1 **Hold the foregrip** on the rod firmly, and insert the reel foot into the groove at the bottom of the grip.

2 **Tighten the locking rings** against the reel foot, to secure the reel in place. They should be finger tight.

ATTACHING A CONVENTIONAL REEL

A conventional reel is attached on top of the rod, and this is the position in which it is used during fishing. The reel seat on the rod has grooves, into which the foot of the reel is placed. It is secured in position with locking rings.

1 Place the foot of the reel into the grooves on the reel seat, while holding on tightly to the reel.

2 Screw the locking rings tightly into place, and make sure there is no play in the reel once they are tight.

LOADING THE LINE

Line loaded onto any reel must be laid under tight and even pressure. Under the strain produced by hard-fighting fish working against a tightly set drag, loose coils of line can bed down into the reel and may snap. Some reels have an automatic level-wind system (*see below*).

1 Tie the line around the spool with a secure knot, such as the blood or uni knot (*see* pp.31, 32).

2 Tighten the knot close to the spool, and then trim the loose end with a pair of cutters.

3 Wind the reel to take up the line while holding it under tension. This is easier to do with a helper.

4 Use your thumb to act as a guide to spread the line evenly across the spool of the reel from one side to the other.

5 Wind the line on evenly. This will help with trouble-free casting, and will allow the fish to run.

6 When you are filling a reel for long-distance casting, make sure not to overfill it. Leave a ⅛-in (2-mm) gap at the top of the spool.

Line wound evenly across full width of the spool

LEVEL-WIND SYSTEM

Many conventional reels come with a level-wind system that automatically spreads the line evenly over the spool. While this is by far the easiest, and often the most effective, way to wind line onto a conventional reel (especially when using thin-diameter braid), reels without a level wind offer longer casting.

Level-wind mechanism

Types of reels

There are three major types of fishing reels: spinning, conventional, and fly reel. Within each of these categories there are freshwater and saltwater fishing versions. A baitcasting reel is essentially a smaller conventional reel that is better suited to casting.

FRESHWATER REELS

Spinning reels are most commonly used in freshwater fishing. This type of reel is easy to use and highly effective in many situations, and will work well with light lures and small baits. However, for casting larger lures, baitcasting reels are a popular choice. When used correctly, conventional reels offer a more direct action and precision casting.

Large conventional reels are used in more demanding freshwater locations and for big fish, such as mahseer and Nile perch. These strong fish demand the use of powerful tackle.

Bale arm

Handle grip

MEDIUM SPINNING REEL
A larger reel body, increased spool capacity, and stronger gearing allow for much larger fish to be landed on a reel like this.

SPINNING REEL HANDLE
Most spinning reels offer the angler the option of changing the handle to the left-hand or right-hand side.

Reel foot

SMALL SPINNING REEL
With the capacity to hold only a small amount of line, a small spinning reel is designed for taking small fish on a light rod.

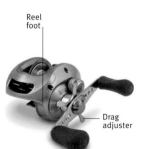

Reel foot

Drag adjuster

LOW-PROFILE BAITCASTER
Designed to sit close to the rod, this small baitcasting reel is ideal for precision fishing with light lures. An internal braking system controls the spool during the cast.

Level-wind system

ROUND BAITCASTING REEL
Performing a job similar to the low-profile baitcaster (*left*), some baitcasting reels are strong enough to tackle big fish in freshwater or saltwater.

SALTWATER REELS

Specialty saltwater reels are made from materials that incorporate resistance to corrosion from salt. They range from small spinning reels right through to the largest big-game fishing conventional reels, which are designed to hold huge quantities of heavy line and deal with hard-fighting fish. For this type of fishing, a heavy-duty reel that has an effective drag system enables the angler to play and land the largest specimens.

Spool-release lever

Drag adjuster

Handle

SMALL CONVENTIONAL REEL
Many smaller conventional and baitcasting reels have a braking mechanism that slows the spool when you are casting. This prevents overruns and tangles.

MEDIUM CONVENTIONAL REEL
A large line capacity and strong construction make these reels suitable for heavier fishing. Many also have a braking system (*see left*).

Reel stem

Spool

Body casing

Reel foot

LARGE CONVENTIONAL REEL
Big conventional reels built for heavy-duty boat-fishing are extremely robust. Many have smooth lever-drag systems able to deal with very fast, powerful fish.

MEDIUM SPINNING REEL
Well suited to long, smooth casts with lures, this type of reel works well for spinning and light bait-fishing. It can be filled with monofilament or braid line.

LARGE SPINNING REEL
Popular with shore-anglers, spinning reels can cope with heavy lines and large fish. They are also easier to use than conventional reels.

FLY REELS

Modern fly-fishing reels appear to be intricately engineered, but inside they are usually simple. Large fly reels incorporate drag systems, but they are rarely geared in the same way as a conventional or spinning reel. The size of fly reel you choose is governed by the potential size of the fish and the weight of your line. They are usually rated by weight according the AFTM's system used for fly rods and lines. Choose a reel that is compatible with the rod and the weight of line you wish to use.

Handle

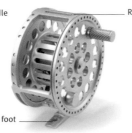

Reel cage

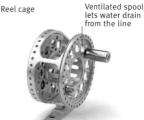

Ventilated spool lets water drain from the line

Reel foot

LARGE SALTWATER FLY REEL
Designed to hold large quantities of line, this reel can be used to catch big fish. Reels of this type incorporate a drag system.

SALMON-FISHING FLY REEL
Modern salmon-fishing reels are more robust and larger than standard fly reels. They hold large quantities of line.

SMALL-RIVER FLY REEL
These reels are light but very strong. They are best for small rivers and lakes, where the targets are usually trout and grayling.

Hooks and weights

Hooks and weights are the main elements of what is collectively termed "terminal tackle." The hook is your final and crucial link with the fish, and usually, your line will not reach the fish without a weight. Spend time working out which types suit your fishing best.

HOOK BASICS

The most widely used hook is the single J-hook, but many lures carry triple hooks, and some salmon flies are tied on double hooks. For freshwater fishing, a spade-end hook is sometimes used (a hook with no eye, just a flattened end), but most hooks have an eye through which you attach your trace or leader (*see* pp.32–33). The gauge refers to the diameter of the wire from which a hook is made. Heavier-gauge hooks are used for larger fish, and to help sink flies.

HOOK SIZES
Sizes are denoted by numbers, with the largest number being the smallest hook, from a size 30 up to a size 1. Hooks larger than a size 1 adopt a zero after the first number, with larger numbers denoting larger hooks—such as 2/o. The examples below are actual size.

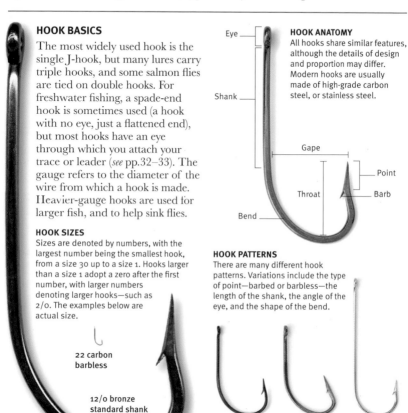

22 carbon barbless

12/o bronze standard shank

HOOK ANATOMY
All hooks share similar features, although the details of design and proportion may differ. Modern hooks are usually made of high-grade carbon steel, or stainless steel.

Eye
Shank
Gape
Point
Throat
Barb
Bend

HOOK PATTERNS
There are many different hook patterns. Variations include the type of point—barbed or barbless—the length of the shank, the angle of the eye, and the shape of the bend.

Circular   Semicircular   Longshank

SALTWATER HOOKS

Hooks used in saltwater fishing need to have some corrosion resistance, whether this is a coating applied to the hook or the use of a material such as stainless steel. Points are often chemically sharpened, to provide efficient hooking. Choose a size and shape that will cope with your target. For sea fishing, these often need to be immensely powerful to deal with big fish that fight hard. Circle hooks (*right*) are used when ease of unhooking is important.

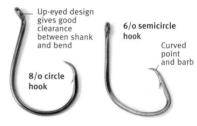

Up-eyed design gives good clearance between shank and bend

8/o circle hook

6/o semicircle hook

Curved point and barb

CIRCLE HOOKS
Designed to hook fish so that they are easy to release, circle hooks prevent deep hooking, which may damage the fish.

FRESHWATER HOOKS

Many freshwater hooks are small, but can deal with surprisingly large fish, and there is a range of shapes for bait-, lure-, and fly-fishing. Fly-fishing hooks vary widely, to cater to fly patterns requiring different styles of hooks (*see* pp.42–47).

Fine-gauge wire

Down-eyed design gives better penetration on the strike

Longshank carp hook

Wide-gape carp hook

CARP HOOKS
There are numerous hooks available for carp fishing, in different shapes, sizes, and gauges, for a variety of conditions.

TREBLE HOOKS
A treble hook has three points and is usually encountered as part of a lure in which a standard hook could be obscured. Many lures only work when used with treble hooks. They can be hard to remove.

BARBLESS HOOKS

The barb holds the hook in place when a fish is caught, and sometimes they can make a hook difficult to remove. A barbless hook slips out very easily. Many anglers choose to use this design for this reason, and many fisheries have regulations that specify the use of barbless hooks, especially where there is a catch-and-release policy.

Bulldawg freshwater lure

Treble hook

WEIGHTS

Weights on a fishing rig are used for many tasks, from anchoring a bait on the bottom, to setting the depth (known as "cocking") of a float. Other functions of weights include keeping baits at the desired depth, helping them roll around in the tide or current, and helping lures go deeper. Different shapes of weight perform different tasks.

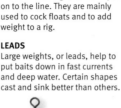

SPLIT SHOT
These small weights are crimped on to the line. They are mainly used to cock floats and to add weight to a rig.

LEADS
Large weights, or leads, help to put baits down in fast currents and deep water. Certain shapes cast and sink better than others.

GRIP LEAD WITH A BAIT CLIP
A grip lead has spikes to anchor it to the sea bed. When you come to retrieve, the spikes break out of the bottom and the lead comes in. A bait clip behind the hook helps to protect baits during the cast, and improves aerodynamics.

Additional terminal tackle

The main function of terminal tackle, which is attached to the end of your line, is to present your baits, or to work your lures, more efficiently. Your link to the fish will be weakened by poorly chosen terminal tackle. Use the best-quality components you can afford.

SWIVELS AND CRIMPS

Use swivels to join lines that do not have to pass through rod rings. They come in various sizes, and the eyes rotate in the swivel body to help prevent line twist when casting. Three-way swivels may be weak, but used correctly they can tie a dropper off the trace. Crimps secure heavy mono line or wire that cannot be tied. Pass line through the crimp, through the eye of the swivel or hook, and then back through the crimp. Squeeze the crimp closed with pliers or a crimping tool.

3-way swivel

2-way swivel

CRIMPS
Crimps can be used to stop and trap swivels on a trace, for making long dropper rigs.

SWIVELS
Two-way swivels come in barrel and stronger, ball-bearing types (shown). Three-way swivels are usually barrel-type, and have a larger size-to-strength ratio.

A SIMPLE RIG

The rig is the collective term used for terminal tackle: the weights, hooks, swivels, swimfeeders, and other components that you tie on to catch the fish. Lure setups tend not to be called part of a rig, whereas anything involving a baited hook is. Some rigs are intricate, to aid bait presentation and casting, and some include up to three hooks.

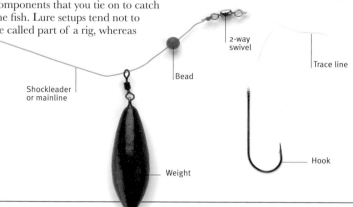

2-way swivel

Trace line

Bead

Shockleader or mainline

Weight

Hook

BAIT CLIPS

Clips are used in saltwater fishing to tuck bait close to the trace when distance casting; they release on impact with the sea. Clips reduce wind resistance, so the rig will cast farther. They also protect soft baits, especially worms, that may become damaged in distance casting. Clipping the bait down also makes it easier to cast long traces, because the extra line cannot flap around.

BREAKAWAY CLIP
The bait clips behind the plastic dome. When it hits the water, the impact drives the dome up and away from the leader, which ejects the baited hook.

Floats

There is a huge range of floats on the market, each designed to work in a specific type of water. To choose a float, read the notes on the packaging, or ask in the tackle shop for the floats most suitable to your fishing. Carry a selection in a crushproof box.

THE FUNCTION OF FLOATS

A float is a means of suspending a bait at a specific depth—either on the surface, under the surface, or on the bottom. It also gives a visual signal when a fish hits your bait. If the float twitches erratically, shoots under, or comes up suddenly and lies flat on the surface, you have a bite. Most floats need some kind of weighting to get them to cock properly, but some are self-weighted or require no weight because the bait is heavy enough to make it work.

RIGGING A FLOAT
Most floats sit above the trace, fixed or sliding into place via weighted stops that fish the bait at the required depth. The weight cocks the float upright.

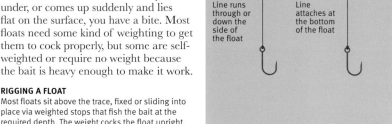

Line runs through or down the side of the float

Line attaches at the bottom of the float

USING FRESHWATER FLOATS

Sometimes you will want your float to remain in one position on a lake, perhaps over groundbait, whereas on a river it is usual to let the float work with the current to cover more ground. It is helpful to place two or three of the required split shot close to the bottom of the float, and then put the rest closer to the hook to help the float fish correctly.

FRESHWATER FLOAT-FISHING
Floats used for freshwater fishing come in a wide range of shapes and sizes. Make sure to pick one that best suits your fishing.

USING SALTWATER FLOATS

Floats will help to put your baits (and lures at times) in places where you could not possibly cast. Saltwater floats are generally larger, and less varied, than freshwater floats, as they have to support larger baits. Aim to drift your float in the current when possible, to cover more ground where the fish might be.

SALTWATER FLOAT-FISHING
Floats with a round shape will support larger baits, such as crabs and fish for tarpon bait. Many specialty floats cock purely from the weight of the bait.

Lines and knots

Line is the main element that connects you to the fish you hook. Mainline is the bulk line on your reel, and your leader (or shockleader) is tied to the end of it. A trace (or hooklength) is the shorter line tied to the hook. Fly lines are different, and must have a leader attached that holds the fly.

TYPES OF MAINLINES

The principal types of mainlines are mono (monofilament), braided, and fly lines. For fly-fishing, light flies need a weighted fly line to impart momentum, or casting weight, to get the fly out onto or into the water. The relatively short main fly line is then joined to a long length of backing line (braid or specialty backing material).

MONO LINES

Used for freshwater and sea fishing, monofilament line is good for long casting, and its inherent stretch gives shock-absorbency for landing fish.

LINE CHOICES

Mono and braided lines are available in a range of strengths and are rated by breaking strain and line diameter. Heavier lines, which are often used as shockleaders (see p.34), tend to come in shorter lengths and on smaller spools than mono and braid mainlines. Fly lines are rated according to the AFTM code, where a line is given a specific weight, such as #8.

FLY LINES

A fly line consists of an insert line and a coating. Some are designed to float, some to sink slowly (intermediate), some to sink quickly, and some to sink at different speeds, from medium to ultra-fast.

THREADING FLY LINE

A useful trick for threading fly line onto the rod is to double the line over and then push it through the rod rings. This will drag the leader behind the fly line, pulling it through the rings. Mono and braid lines will be damaged if doubled over, and must be threaded through in a single strand.

Fly line pushed through ring

BRAIDED LINES

Braids have a high strength-to-diameter ratio, allowing thinner, lighter lines to be used to cut through tide and wind. Care must be taken as they do not stretch like mono. The lack of stretch provides a very direct contact with hooked fish.

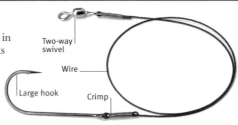

WIRE TRACES

Wire mainline used to be popular in deep water and fast tides, where its small diameter could cut through the water with little resistance. Braided lines now perform this function, and wire is now used mainly when angling for fish with sharp teeth. Some wire traces can be tied almost as easily as mono. Heavier wires require either crimping or a special knot.

SHARK TRACE
A typical shark-type trace consists of a big hook and a swivel, joined by a durable wire trace that is crimped at both ends.

BLOOD KNOT

Also called the half-blood knot, this is the most basic of fishing knots, used to tie line to items such as hooks, swivels, and lures. It is also commonly used to tie together two lines of similar diameter. It will work effectively for many fishing applications. Most anglers will quickly learn a variety of knots.

A HOOK JOINED TO A LINE
The blood knot provides a neat way of securing a hook to a line. It is secure under tension.

1 Take the line through the eye of the hook, swivel, or lure, and then loop the end around the line at least five times.

2 Pass the end that has been looped around the line back through the gap that is left between the eye and the first loop.

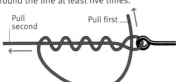

3 Lubricate the whole knot by applying saliva. Pull the short end through (but not tightly), and then pull steadily on the other end.

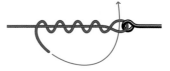

4 Ease the coils down with a steady, non-jerky pull, to form the knot. Trim the end close to the knot, but leave a tag sticking out.

SURGEON'S KNOT

This alternative knot for joining two lines that are of unequal diameter is especially useful in fly-fishing, where you may need to join lines of different breaking strains.

Surgeon's knot

1 Lay both lines side-by-side with the tag ends facing in opposite directions. Keeping the lines together, form a loop. Pass both lines through the loop twice.

2 Moisten and pull the knot tight by pulling both ends simultaneously. Trim the tag ends short with a pair of scissors or sharp clippers.

SHOCKLEADER KNOT

When casting with heavy lures and weights, use a strong knot to join a length of stronger line, known as a shockleader, to your weaker mainline. The shockleader protects the mainline from the shock of the cast. Also known as a hooklength, or trace, a leader is generally shorter, and is used to provide protection against rough-skinned fish and fish with powerful teeth.

SHOCKLEADER KNOT
The shockleader knot is useful for joining thick shockleaders and thin mainlines. The knot has a low profile that will pass easily through the rod rings.

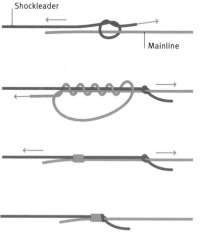

1 **Make a loose overhand** knot in the shockleader. Pull a length of mainline through the middle of the overhand knot.

2 **Loop the mainline** over and around the shockleader to form a uni knot (*see below*). Ensure that the turns enclose both lines.

3 **Moisten both knots.** Tighten the overhand knot in the shockleader, and ease the coils of the uni knot together by pulling the tag end.

4 **Ease the knots together** (moisten the knots again if necessary) and then trim the knots very close to leave very small tag ends.

UNI KNOT

An extremely versatile and strong knot, the uni knot is simple to tie and has a range of uses. When fully tightened, it can be used as an alternative to the blood knot. It can also be used as a loop knot by pulling the tag tight just before the knot pulls all the way down. Joining one uni knot to another is a great way to join two lines of similar diameter, but be sure to ease each knot gently into place.

JOINING LINE TO A SWIVEL
One of the main applications of this multipurpose knot is to join line securely to a swivel or hook. Be sure to trim the tag end neatly.

Trim tag end

1 **Take the line** through the eye of the swivel and form a loop by bringing it back toward the eye. Make several turns inside the loop and around both strands of line.

2 **Gently pull the tag end** of the line so that the knot closes but is not tight. This will form the knot a little way from the eye of the swivel.

3 **Ease the knot** (moisten with saliva if necessary) close to the eye of the swivel and then pull both ends until the knot is tight. Trim the tag end close to the eye.

BLOOD LOOP

Also known as a dropper loop, this knot creates a fixed loop at right angles to your line onto which you can attach a lure or hook. While there are stronger variations, the basic knot described below is easy to tie and works well for many fishing applications.

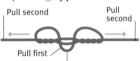

1 **Make a loop** in your line of approximately the required size of the finished loop. Then wrap the loop around itself several times. Take the middle of the loop through the center section of the coils that you have created.

2 **Pull the loop** through to form a new loop. Moisten the knot and then pull both ends of the line gently.

3 **Ease the coils together** tightly to secure the finished loop.

USING A BLOOD LOOP
Thread the hook or lure onto the loop, or cut the loop and attach the item with a blood or uni knot.

RAPALA KNOT

The Rapala knot is an effective method of forming a loop for the lure, hook, or fly, allowing it to move more freely and naturally than if secured by a knot that is tight to the eye. Make the initial loop large enough to allow the knot to be formed well away from the eye. Remember to ease the knot up slowly, and moisten it before doing so. The perfection loop and nonslip mono knots can also be used for this purpose.

ATTACHING A LURE
Many lures fish more effectively when attached to a line with a Rapala knot. This type of knot gives the lure more freedom of movement in the water.

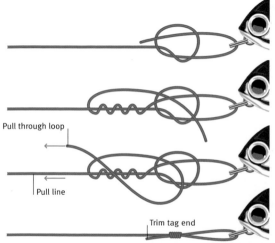

Pull through loop

Pull line

Trim tag end

1 **Tie a loose** overhand knot in the line and pull the free end through it and the lure eye, and back through the knot.

2 **Wrap the free end** three times around the line and take it back through the original overhand loop.

3 **Feed the free end** through the loop that has been formed from the previous step. Tighten the knot.

4 **When you have** pulled the knot tight, trim the tag end neatly.

Baits

The variety of freshwater baits available to anglers is huge, so take time to choose the correct bait to use for the type of fishing you intend to do. Many baits work by introducing fish-attracting smells into the water, so make sure your baits are as fresh as possible.

FRESHWATER BAITS

Natural baits are often freely available if you are prepared to collect your own—most anglers dig for worms at some time. Many tackle shops will stock a selection of popular local baits, such as worms and fish baits, both live and frozen.

Many freshwater baits can be stored in the refrigerator in bait boxes that have perforated lids to allow air in. When you go fishing, take them in a cooler to protect them against temperature extremes.

Some fish (especially big carp) become wise to natural baits, so these baits work best where the fish have not experienced serious angling pressure. Carry a selection of natural baits and take enough to enable you to throw in offerings (little and often). This is like using groundbait, a mixture designed to spread out in the water and attract fish via its scent and visual appeal.

PROCESSED BAITS

Freshwater baits that are not part of a fish's natural food may include items from our own diet—bread, corn, cheese, and processed meats—as well as dog

LIVEBAITS
Many predatory freshwater fish can be caught using a variety of locally sourced livebaits.

biscuits, seeds, and grains. There are also specially made high-protein processed baits. Originally designed solely for carp fishing, these baits are now proving successful in a variety of everyday freshwater angling. High-protein baits are manufactured from a mixture of animal proteins, soy flour, eggs, flavorings, and colorings, and their various smells and flavors are incredible.

KEEP YOUR BAITS AT HAND
When fishing for spooky fish close to the bank, have your baits spread around you where you can easily swing your rig in and rebait while staying in the same position.

LIVE SHRIMP
A neatly hooked shrimp can prove irresistable to many saltwater species. Snook especially respond well to shrimp.

them far less appealing and they will lose their fresh smell. As you want a pleasant natural scent coming from the baits, be careful of taking them out in hot weather. Invest in a cooler to keep them as cold as possible, and keep them out of direct sunlight. Bait scent is gradually washed away, so change baits often, even if you are not getting any bites. Softer baits, such as worms, need changing more frequently. Putting a juicy scent trail into the water via your baits is like groundbaiting; chum (a mixture of fish, blood, fish oil, and perhaps bran) and other free offerings are also often used.

SALTWATER BAITS

There are four basic categories of saltwater bait: fish (whole fish, sections, fillets, and strips), worms, crustaceans (crabs, shrimp, and so on), and livebait (various species of fish), as well as regional specialties. Some areas have regulations against using certain baits—ask in your tackle shop and check the Internet for up-to-date advice.

Research the fish you are targeting—knowing what they feed on will increase your catch rates, especially as different fish species show marked preferences for particular baits, often varying according to the time of year.

Base the sizes of your baits on the size of your prey and the size of its mouth, and on how far you need to cast the bait. Big baits may catch big fish, but so can small baits, and they also catch lots of smaller fish.

CARING FOR AND USING BAITS

Take care of your baits at home and when you go fishing. Do not let frozen baits defrost unless you are about to use them; defrosting and refreezing make

LIVE MACKEREL
Feather rigs are used to catch mackerel for fresh bait. They may be used for livebaits, but are hard to keep alive. Frozen mackerel are a good alternative to fresh ones.

Lures

A lure is an imitation of a baitfish, designed to provoke an attack from a predatory fish. There are many lures available, so seek advice and consider what will appeal to your target fish, taking into account the lure's color, size, the depth at which it works, and the way it moves.

HOW LURES WORK

Lures are usually made of metal, plastic, or wood, but modern designs made of soft plastic are also popular. Lures are designed to work in different ways, but it is the angler who, by constantly working the line, must impart "life" to them. Without this, they remain an inert and uninteresting imitation that will not appeal to any fish. One of the great attractions of lure-fishing is that the angler is always active and is therefore highly involved in the process of fishing.

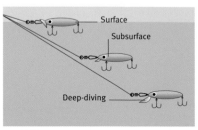

LURE DEPTHS
Lures swim at particular depths to appeal to specific predators. The design of the vane, or blade, of the lure often determines the depth at which it works.

TYPES OF FRESHWATER LURES

As with all types of lures, freshwater lures mimic the appearance and swimming patterns of various freshwater baitfish. Some lures are designed to imitate healthy baitfish swimming normally, whereas others are intended to mimic distressed or injured prey, to make them even more attractive to a predator. To use lures successfully, it is important to learn as much as you can about the species you are targeting, and to discover what will make them most likely to want to charge into your lure.

SURFACE LURES

Some surface lures work on the water surface, where the predator will spy them from below, and cannot sink. Others are designed to float until the angler begins to retrieve, at which point they will dive down to a specific depth.

Angle of the blade keeps lure at the surface

Bass-a-Rooney

SUBSURFACE LURES

Designed to swim under the surface, most subsurface lures do not dive very deep. Some work most effectively on a steady retrieve, while others demand a twitched, jerky retrieve that gets them moving erratically.

Angle and size of the blade keep lure just below the surface

Zalt Zam

DEEP-DIVING LURES

Lures that work at depth are either weighted, or the angle of the blade drives them down as they are retrieved. Make sure your lure will not swim deeper than the water's depth—losing lures through snagging is expensive.

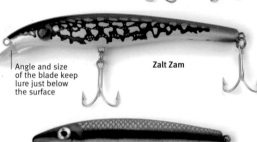

Angle of the blade causes the lure to dive

Ernie

CHOOSING A LURE

Without doubt, many lures are designed more to attract the angler than the fish, but over time you will learn which lures work best for which fish, and under which conditions. Some fish show a marked preference for certain colors; for example, barracuda like a red and white combination. Dark lures often work best in dull conditions and bright lures work better when the light is brighter. If a fish swirls at your lure but does not connect, stop the retrieve for a second and see if the fish comes back. If it does not, aim to cover the same area with your next cast. Give a lure plenty of time to work and do not change it too hastily. Your confidence in the lure you have selected is all-important.

MAKING A SELECTION
Anglers usually carry all manner of different lures, but will tend to return to the one with which they have had most success in the past.

SPINNERS AND SPOONS

These lures are often made of metal. A spinner is designed to spin in the water when retrieved; light often bounces off its shiny sides to further entice a predator. When using a spinner, make sure you have a swivel in your trace as this will help to counteract line twist. Spoons are very similar to spinners, but they usually wobble and jerk erratically when retrieved, rather than simply spin.

Hornet spinner

Treble hook

Taimenlippa spinner spoon

Professor spoon

JERKBAIT LURES

Available in both hard and soft materials, and in surface and subsurface designs, jerkbait lures are cast out and twitched back. A short, strong rod is needed to cope with the large lure and its jerky movements.

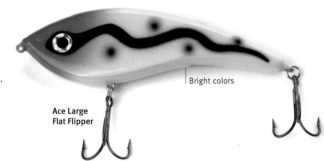

Bright colors

Ace Large
Flat Flipper

SALTWATER FISHING WITH LURES

From the shallowest inshore waters to the blue depths offshore where the biggest species roam, the oceans contain plenty of predatory fish that will readily take lures. It is the variety in saltwater lure-fishing that makes it so special. Whereas bait-fishing is about casting or dropping your bait and waiting for the fish to come to you (sight-fishing excepted), lure-

HOOKED PERFECTLY
A small lure known as a jig is worked along the bottom, often acting like a moving shrimp. A jig has successfully hooked this fish.

fishing involves working your lures to fool the fish. Among the most exciting moments you can experience in angling is the sudden jolt as a fish hits your sinking lure or the great swirl of water as a fish charges your surface lure.

TYPES OF SALTWATER LURE

Like freshwater lures, saltwater lures are designed to work at different depths, although many of the big predators are happy to hit surface lures too. Top-water angling is very popular, especially in warmer tropical seas, as these contain the most species to fish for using this

approach. Surface and just subsurface lures are also excellent for rough ground, where a deep-diving lure would get snagged. Some big-game species can be caught using these lures, such as marlin and tuna, which are often caught just under or very near the surface on trolled lures.

SURFACE LURES

Surface lures come in a variety of shapes and sizes and are all designed to create a degree of water-surface disturbance, which sends out what appear to be distress signals to hungry predators. Poppers have an incurving front that can be made to spit water to imitate an injured baitfish. Others are weighted in such a way as to enable the angler to "walk" them across the surface by moving the rod tip back and forth—known as "walking the dog."

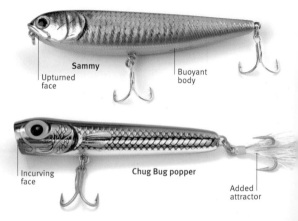

Sammy
Upturned face

Buoyant body

Incurving face

Chug Bug popper

Added attractor

SUBSURFACE LURES

These attract a variety of fish, even the big-game species. Be aware that they can pick up weeds or floating debris, which kills their action. With practice you will know when the lure is not working.

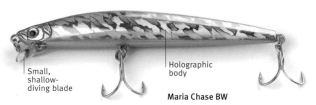

Small, shallow-diving blade

Holographic body

Maria Chase BW

DEEP-DIVING LURES

Often trolled from boats, many deep-diving lures also work well when cast conventionally from the shore or a boat. Check that the water is deep enough.

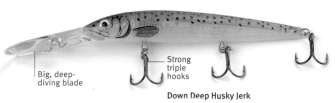

Big, deep-diving blade

Strong triple hooks

Down Deep Husky Jerk

VERTICAL JIGS

Butterfly or vertical jigs are used in deep water for fast-moving tropical game species. They are dropped to the bottom and then jerked up and down.

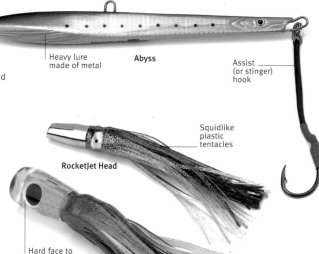

Heavy lure made of metal

Abyss

Assist (or stinger) hook

Squidlike plastic tentacles

RocketJet Head

TROLLING LURES

Designed primarily for the big-game species, such as marlin, these often big and colorful lures are trolled in particular patterns on outriggers behind boats. Many are intended to be fished with live or dead bait that sits behind the lure's "head," often on a pair of large hooks.

Hard face to disturb water surface

Marlin Super Shaker

SOFT PLASTICS

Many natural baits have been imitated by these flexible, sometimes scented lures. These designs vibrate and make realistic movements, which appeal to a wide range of fish. The famous jellyworm and shad patterns are used with and without weights.

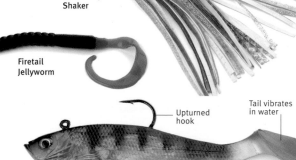

Firetail Jellyworm

Tail vibrates in water

Upturned hook

Wild Eye Shad

Fly basics

Flies are made from a variety of natural and synthetic materials, to create an illusion of life that fools the fish. When fly-fishing, you need to carry a selection of fly designs, or patterns, that will entice the fish, chosen according to the habitat and diet of the target species.

ATTRACTORS AND DECEIVERS

Flies are often categorized as either attractors or deceivers. Attractors are usually brightly colored, with lots of mobility arousing an aggressive feeding instinct in the fish. Deceivers work by imitating a specific food item that will interest the fish. When stocking a fly box, be sure to add a variety of flies designed to both attract and deceive.

SQUID PINK
This pattern has the outline of a squid, but its bright pink coloring does not resemble the natural creature, so it is classed as an attractor.

FISH FRY
Flies do not always imitate airborne food items. The Surf Candy fly (*right*) is designed to look just like a small baitfish, and would be used when fly-fishing for saltwater species, such as bass.

6-day-old fish fry

Surf Candy fly

DADDY LONGLEGS
Trout love the crane-flies that hatch in large numbers during the fall. The artificial Daddy Longlegs fly mimics the delicate wings and gangly legs of the natural fly perfectly, and is a great example of a fly designed to deceive.

Adult crane fly

Daddy Longlegs fly

Adult Mayfly fly

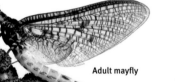

Adult mayfly

MAYFLIES
Fly anglers look forward to the seasonal hatch of mayflies, which often triggers a gluttonous response from species such as trout. Mayfly fly patterns mimic the key features of the natural insect, such as the long tail, barred abdomen, and characteristic wings.

TYING YOUR OWN FLIES

There is something deeply satisfying about tying your own flies, and it saves money—professionally tied flies can be expensive. Examples of basic materials include pheasant tail feathers, rabbit fur, and thin wire. There are many companies offering fly-tying resources for sale; for a beginner, it is worth investing in a basic kit incorporating a number of useful materials, hooks, and a few fly patterns with instructions on how to tie them. Practice tying flies at a well-lit bench, and tie several of the same pattern until you master it. Don't worry if your first attempts are a bit scruffy and not like the pictures shown; the fish will probably accept them.

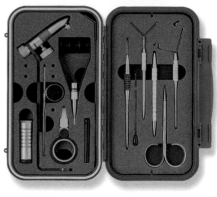

FLY-TYING KIT
You will need a number of tools to tie flies, including a vise to clamp the hook, a bobbin to hold your tying thread, and a pair of sharp scissors to cut materials.

ANATOMY OF A FLY

Fly patterns incorporate a number of features; some flies have all the features, while others possess only a few. Learn the techniques required to tie each part of the pattern shown here, and you will be well equipped to create a wide-ranging supply of artificial flies for your box. In general, flies are constructed from the bend of the hook toward the eye, and completed at the head.

Wing

Head

Tail

Rib

Hackle

Hook

TYING A FLY

Fly tying requires concentration, a steady hand, and good lighting. The fly-tying vise should be set at a comfortable height, and sharp scissors are essential for success.

A SALTWATER FLY
The pattern being made here will imitate a saltwater shrimp. The body is spun fur, bound on to the hook using a process known as "dubbing."

Types of flies

When you choose a fly, take into account the depth at which the fish are usually located, and the food upon which they generally feed. Artificial flies are split into two groups: subsurface patterns, which are called wet flies, and surface patterns, which are known as dry flies.

FRESHWATER WET FLIES

Wet flies are intended to imitate a range of fish food found under water, such as the pupae of flies ascending to the surface, or nymphs and larvae often found near the bed of lakes or rivers. Some wet flies are designed to look very much like small fish and even various crustaceans, such as shrimp.

Wet flies often incorporate some kind of weight to assist their descent. A sinking fly line is used to fish them at a variety of depths. When using a wet fly you will often be unable to see the fly while fishing, and will, therefore, need to feel for a take or watch the fly line for signs of a fish. You can also try fishing a group of wet flies together on a leader. This tactic will allow you to position the patterns at a range of depths, increasing your chance of success.

SUPER BUZZER SUPREME (OLIVE)
Much of the trout's diet consists of midges (also known as "buzzers"). The Super Buzzer imitates the midge pupae.

DEPTH CHARGE CZECH MATES
This fast-sinking artificial, which was designed by Czech anglers, will fool fish feeding deep down on caddis-fly larvae.

DAMSEL NYMPH (MEDIUM OLIVE)
Trout rarely take the adult damsel but cannot resist the nymph, which moves with an enticing wiggle. Olive is a favored color.

DABBLER (CLARET)
Traditional wet flies, such as the Dabbler, imitate semi-hatched or drowning flies, and often have a feathery outline called a hackle.

HARE'S-EAR NYMPH
This versatile design is almost guaranteed to catch fish that feed on a variety of insects and crustaceans all year round.

FRESHWATER DRY FLIES

Dry flies can be used to attract the fish either by imitating a natural fly, or by disturbing the surface of the water. They are tied on lightweight hooks and incorporate features that will assist their buoyancy. Among the enormous variety of top-of-the-water patterns, some mimic insects as they hatch and others resemble those that are stranded on the surface after hatching. There are also designs that mimic a fly that has reproduced and has now fallen into the water.

If your dry fly starts to sink, retrieve it and dry it with tissue paper and apply some floatant. This can be purchased at a tackle shop in the form of a liquid, spray, or gel.

Observe your surroundings carefully when fishing with dry flies. In particular, look for insects on the water, hiding in vegetation, and flying in the air. Try to match these findings by choosing fly patterns that are similar in appearance. Fish feeding at the surface are often selective and may refuse a fly that does not mimic their chosen prey.

CHERNOBYL ANT
The Chernobyl Ant is an excellent example of an artificial fly with a strong silhouette. It can be fished in rough water, or down and across a river, where it will create an enticing wake.

FRESHWATER FLY-FISHING
Freshwater fish live on a diet of the various stages of development of insects and bugs, which lend themselves to imitation with artificial fly patterns.

ADAM'S PARACHUTE
This famous and effective fly is justly popular and will catch fish on both moving and still water. It is a good general dry fly pattern.

DAD'S DEMOISELLE
Fish rarely take adult damsel flies, as a great deal of energy is needed to catch them. However, it is worth having a copy in case you find an energetic fish!

KLINKHAMMER CADDIS (GREEN)
This is another essential dry fly that sits perfectly in the surface film and imitates an adult caddis- or sedge-fly in the process of hatching out.

HUMPY
The Humpy is particularly useful in rough water as the stiff feather hackle and deer-hair body provide superb buoyancy and a strong silhouette.

F-FLY
This is a simple yet deadly pattern, often called an emerger. The body sits just below the surface and is made buoyant by a duck-feather wing laced with oil.

SALTWATER FLIES

In saltwater fly-fishing, the "fly" patterns that are used to outwit saltwater species take the form of anything but insects. Saltwater "flies" have to mimic a variety of food items including crabs, shrimp, and small fish. To be successful it is important to arm yourself with patterns that replicate the diet of your target.

Take into account the depth to be fished and remember that saltwater habitats vary enormously, so carry flies in a range of sizes, colors, and weights.

Choose appropriate rods and lines, too. Saltwater patterns can be heavy and may require rods rated above line #8 to cope with their weight and create high line speeds to counteract air resistance.

IMITATIVE PATTERNS

Whenever you are purchasing or tying flies that aim directly to imitate the quarry's diet, make sure the artificial pattern reproduces all the essential elements of the natural food, as it is these that can trigger a hit. Fish species that inhabit tropical saltwater flats, such as the bonefish, feed heavily on crustaceans, including shrimp.

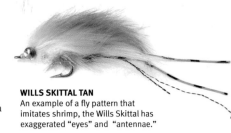

WILLS SKITTAL TAN
An example of a fly pattern that imitates shrimp, the Wills Skittal has exaggerated "eyes" and "antennae."

SQUID WHITE
Imitating its namesake, the Squid White has feathers that mimic tentacles and conspicuous "eyes," features that may provoke a feeding response.

SURF CANDY
Copying the prominent lateral line and forked tail of many juvenile fish, the Surf Candy is highly realistic.

BAITFISH PATTERNS

Numerous predators—including bass and tuna—are attracted to baitfish patterns, and the result is often hectic sport. Simple, lightweight patterns are easy to cast, while lending themselves

to many color variations and sizes that imitate an extensive range of baitfish. For success with baitfish patterns, look for signs of feeding activity, such as diving gulls, and head swiftly to the area, as the frenzied activity can be brief.

GUMMY MINNOW
The translucent synthetic materials used in the Gummy Minnow produce a highly successful pattern.

CLOUSER MINNOW
Incorporating the two-tone livery displayed by many baitfish, the Clouser Minnow's weighted "eyes" ensure that it fishes upside down and clear of snags.

BASS GRIZZLE
An example of a simple lightweight pattern, the Bass Grizzle is a popular and reliable fly.

SURFACE PATTERNS

Commonly known as poppers, surface patterns are designed to create disturbance in the water surface when retrieved. When you choose them, take into account the conditions to be fished, as well as the size of your quarry. The commotion and stream of bubbles that surface patterns produce is particularly attractive to predatory saltwater fish, which home in on them.

PIWI POPPER
A classic example of an all-around hardworking lure, the Piwi Popper has rubber "legs," which create plenty of movement and a strong silhouette.

CREASE FLY
As the Crease Fly, which mimics a fleeing fish, embarks on a seemingly terrified bid for freedom, its broad, flat front produces a tantalizing vibration in the water, which should attract your target species.

BOBS BANGER
A large, cylindrical fly, Bobs Banger is particularly suitable for using on the surface of rough water, where it creates the desired disturbance.

UNUSUAL FLIES

Flies are not always designed to be thought of as natural food by the target species. Many are intended to arouse an aggressive response, rather than a feeding instinct, while others are tied to copy long-established groundbaits, such as sweet corn or even bread. Some people dislike this break with tradition, but many modern-day anglers want to push fly-fishing boundaries to the limit, and this calls for a whole host of unusual flies aimed at a variety of species.

Whatever your target, always carry a range of flies, as it is often the case that when one species is proving difficult, another is more amenable, so long as you have the right mix of fur and feather.

BONIO
Carp love the very buoyant Bonio fly, which is constructed from spun deer hair and designed to resemble dog biscuits, which are proven carp bait.

TEMPLE DOG
Tube flies, such as the Temple Dog, have a mobile three-dimensional dressing that is attractive to salmon and sea trout.

CACTUS BOOBY (ORANGE)
Perhaps one of the most unusual fly patterns, the very buoyant eyes of the Booby give it its name. It is often used with a fast-sinking line popped up off the lake bed.

Cold-weather clothing

Wearing the right clothing when fishing in cold weather will keep you warm, dry, and—most importantly—safe. Modern fishing clothing is easy to wear and offers levels of protection that will enable you to keep fishing in almost any weather.

ON LAND

Clothing requirements in cold weather are the same for freshwater and saltwater. The outer layer needs to be waterproof, to keep you dry and to cut wind chill. Chest waders are a good choice, but in cold weather you must wear some warm layers underneath. A large proportion of body heat is lost through the head, so wear a warm hat, and a scarf or neck warmer. Gloves keep hands warm. Choose fingerless gloves or types that convert between full coverage and fingerless. Footwear depends on where you are fishing, and whether you need to get into the water. Standard rubber boots offer the best waterproofing, but they need lining with thermal socks, and they do not offer a good grip. Fully lined, thermal boots are the best option for really cold weather. Waterproof hiking boots are great for fishing.

LAYERING

Under waterproofs, build up layers of clothing, for layers both trap the heat and allow your skin to "breathe." It is easier to adjust thinner layers than if you wear big, bulky items. The final layer before your waterproofs is often a fleece jacket, which can be your outer layer if the weather is dry.

Woolen hat

Warm layers

Waterproof jacket

Fingerless gloves to keep hands warm but fingers free

Reinforced knee pads

Adjustable pant bottoms

Waterproof bib-and-suspenders overalls

Strong hiking boots

ON A BOAT

Wear a lifejacket or buoyancy aid when boat-fishing; on many fly-fishing lakes and reservoirs this is a regulation. A lifejacket will keep your head above water, face up; a buoyancy aid gives the wearer a degree of buoyancy only, and will not keep you afloat head-up if you are unconscious. Fishing from boats in cold weather requires the same clothing as fishing on land, but because you cannot move around so much, you need to wear extra layers to keep warm. The more protection you have against the elements, the better you will fish.

LIFEJACKET
A modern lifejacket is designed for comfortable wear over long periods. A small gas canister automatically inflates the lifejacket if you fall in the water.

AT SEA

When you are fishing on a boat out at sea, there is little shelter from the weather, and it will always feel colder than on land. Never go fishing on a boat without a lifejacket on board for every person, a minimum safety requirement. Wear layered clothing underneath waterproofs, and bib-and-suspenders waterproof overalls. Choose bright colors so you can be easily spotted if you fall overboard.

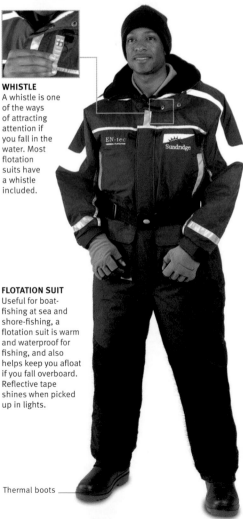

WHISTLE
A whistle is one of the ways of attracting attention if you fall in the water. Most flotation suits have a whistle included.

NEOPRENE CHEST WADERS

Neoprene chest waders are warm, and are ideal for land-based fishing. They combine well with layers, and are available with various sole materials on the underside of the boots. Some have a stocking foot that allows you to wear wading boots. It is not advisable to wear chest waders when boat-fishing.

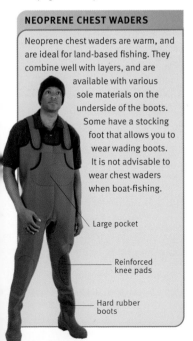

Large pocket

Reinforced knee pads

Hard rubber boots

FLOTATION SUIT
Useful for boat-fishing at sea and shore-fishing, a flotation suit is warm and waterproof for fishing, and also helps keep you afloat if you fall overboard. Reflective tape shines when picked up in lights.

Thermal boots

Warm-weather clothing

When fishing in hot weather, protect yourself against sun and energy-sapping heat. Special fishing clothes, made from modern fabrics, will keep you fishing safely and comfortably in the hottest conditions. If you travel for your fishing, research beforehand what clothes to take.

PREPARATION FOR THE SUN

Check vaccination requirements for your destination, and take insect repellent. Anglers spend long hours with the direct sun overhead and water reflecting the sun's rays; take care in these conditions, and always wear waterproof sunscreen with high UV protection on any exposed skin. Above all, drink plenty of water to keep fully hydrated—drink before you get thirsty, avoiding alcohol and sugary drinks.

Wide-brimmed hat for protection from the sun

Polarized sunglasses

Lightweight cotton shirt

SLEEVE BUTTON
Tropical fishing shirts can be worn long- or short-sleeved. When sleeves are rolled up, they are held in place with buttons or loops.

Sun gloves

Lightweight, quick-drying pants

POCKETS
Zipped and vented pockets store anything from clippers and sunglasses to spare flies.

FLATS PANTS
Ultra-lightweight pants (often called flats pants) are good for warm-weather fishing, with zip-off legs for anglers who prefer shorts. Play it safe with the sun when wearing shorts.

Flats boots

TROPICAL GEAR
A classic tropical fishing outfit offers a high degree of sun protection, but allows the angler unrestricted movement. Back-vented shirts are cool, and modern, breathable materials wick sweat away from the skin. The clothes are made slightly larger than normal to allow for unhindered movement.

ADDITIONAL KIT

The clothing you take depends on where you will be fishing. In the tropics, carry a lightweight waterproof jacket when fishing, ready for sudden downpours. Some warm-weather fishing may be fine with bare feet and, if that is the case, keep applying sunscreen to them, as water and sand wash it off far faster than from the rest of your body. Lightweight boat shoes work well for boat-based fishing, but if you are going to be walking on the flats, always wear flats boots—they help protect you against rocks, coral, stingray barbs, or poisonous, spiny fish buried in the sand. Wrap gravel guards around the tops of your boots to keep sand out. Sun gloves protect your hands. Carry extra fishing tackle in a waterproof boat bag, or a small backpack or fanny pack, and try not to carry unnecessary gear.

FACE PROTECTION
Always wear a hat, to protect your head and shade your eyes. A neck protector or a drop-down back to your hat will protect your neck. In extreme sun you may need to cover your lower face.

SUNGLASSES

Polarized sunglasses serve several distinct purposes. Primarily they serve as fish-spotting tools, to help you see more clearly into the water—polarizing technology works by cutting out glare from the surface of the water, which allows you to see underneath the surface. This is invaluable for spotting fish, and for understanding what lies in front of you. Sunglasses also help to protect your eyes from long periods in sunny conditions, and they act as a barrier against a fly hitting you directly in the eye during a cast.

FLATS BOOTS
Invaluable for wading the flats, these lightweight boots are designed to drain off water when you take your foot out. Hard soles protect the bottoms of your feet from cuts or spikes, and ankle supports help when walking and wading long distances.

Drinking-water pipe

Gravel guards (or long socks turned down)

Fly-fishing clothing

The clothing usually worn for fly-fishing reflects the sport's highly mobile nature. Choose lightweight fabrics, while ensuring that you are prepared for all weather and water conditions. Comfortable anglers enjoy their fishing far more than those at the mercy of the elements!

CLOTHING FOR WADING

Fly-fishing frequently calls for wading, especially in running water. Breathable chest waders provide a durable, lightweight, and waterproof layer that allows freedom of movement and produces minimal perspiration. Waders are available as a boot connected to a pant leg, but the stocking-foot versions, worn with separate footwear, are more versatile and comfortable. Wear a hat to retain warmth; caps with a peak are popular as they reduce glare. Polarized glasses are compulsory fly-fishing attire, protecting your eyes from wayward hooks and assisting subsurface observation. Consider the terrain to be negotiated when choosing a boot sole.

CHEST WADERS AND JACKET
For fly-anglers who want the option of wading, a pair of chest waders and a waterproof jacket are essential items.

GRAVEL GUARD
Worn over waders with separate boots, gravel guards prevent stones from entering the boot and causing discomfort.

FELT SOLES
Choose wading boots with felt soles to provide a secure foothold when fishing in rocky rivers.

Polarized sunglasses

Waterproof pocket

Waterproof, lightweight jacket

Waterproof, breathable chest waders

Gravel guard

Felt-soled wading boots

Carrying your equipment

Anglers always tend to carry a lot of gear, trying to cover as many eventualities as possible. Choosing versatile and convenient ways to transport your equipment is important, as is bearing in mind how far you have to walk or travel to fish when you are packing.

HANDS-FREE CARRYING

A backpack is ideal for transporting your fishing equipment over greater distances, especially if you plan to move around. Choose one that is comfortable to wear for long periods. Chest packs and fanny packs are light and handy for smaller items. Quiver-type rod holdalls are ideal for carrying rods when walking.

BACK AND CHEST PACK

An integrated backpack and chest pack system is especially useful for fly- and lure-fishing. The chest pack unclips so that you can use the backpack separately if you prefer.

FANNY PACK

Very useful for carrying limited equipment over long distances, fanny packs can be worn front or back. The various pockets hold a surprising amount of gear, often plenty for a day's fishing.

FLY VEST

Most fly vests allow you to store essentials, such as flies, leader material, snips, and disgorgers, on the front for easy access. Many have an optional backpack.

Wide webbing spreads load on shoulders

Rigid casings protect flies

FLY BOX

This fly vest incorporates a drop-down fly box. Others have pockets to store small fly boxes. Both are ideal for carrying a selection of flies from your collection.

Essential skills

Unless you are fishing from a boat and can drop your lure or bait directly down into the water, reaching the fish usually involves casting—which requires certain fundamental skills that you need to learn to get started. Hooking, playing, and landing fish are what you do every time a fish bites, and you need to know how to release your catch to enable it to swim away unharmed.

Basic casting

Casting is the means by which anglers propel the bait, lure, or fly to the fish, whether they are close to shore or farther out. There are many variations on casting, but—in both freshwater and saltwater fishing—virtually all are based on the overhead cast.

GETTING YOUR BAIT WHERE YOU WANT IT

Whenever fish are feeding farther out than the length of your fishing rod, a cast is needed to reach them. Your cast will usually require a combination of controlled power and accuracy, and, with practice, this will enable you to place your baits or lures almost exactly where you want them to go.

Casting relies on momentum. It works by compressing the fishing rod to build up power, then releasing the power during the cast, which straightens out or "unwinds" the rod, catapulting your bait or lure out onto the water. You hold

the fishing line in place on the reel until the point of release (*see* step 4, *opposite*) and by then letting go, you allow your bait or lure to fly out, dragging the mainline behind it. Close-range casts—consisting of little more than a quick overhead, sideways, or even underhand flick—are also often needed.

There is no right or wrong way to cast, but make sure you are comfortable and relaxed and be ready to apply power, while staying steady on your feet. Aim for a smooth build-up of power, then release the line.

SPEED AND PRECISION
The overhead cast can be fast or slow to regulate the power. Many casters look at the rod as it comes through, then turn their head as it "unwinds."

MAKING AN OVERHEAD CAST

The overhead cast consists of placing the rod behind you with the lure or weight dangling off the end (have a drop of at least 24 in/60 cm), turning to look at where you want to release, and then bringing the rod around under pressure to bend it and cast. The faster you bring the rod around and the harder you "punch and pull," the farther you cast.

1 **Stand comfortably** with the rod behind you. With your top hand held behind you on the rod, hold the line with your thumb (conventional or baitcasting reel) or index finger (spinning reel).

THUMB CLAMP
Set conventional or baitcasting reels in free-spool mode and stop the reel with your thumb. Release it as you release the cast.

2 **"Punch" the rod** through its arc with your top hand, and "pull" the butt down into your chest or stomach with the lower hand. Keep looking up and aim to really compress (bend) the rod.

3 **The acute bend** in the rod unwinds very suddenly as the rod moves through its arc, and catapults the lead or lure out to the fish. Try to keep your head relatively still through the cast, looking up at about 45 degrees. Remain firm in your stance, with your front leg holding you in position, straightening it if necessary.

4 **As the rod reaches** an angle of about 45 degrees in front, its compression will rapidly unwind. Stay in position, your bottom hand keeping the rod butt down into your chest or stomach, with the top hand holding firm. Lift your thumb or index finger to release line from the reel.

Roll casting

The roll cast is the principal casting method for novice fly-anglers. It is a relatively simple cast that must be learned in order to cope with a range of everyday fly-fishing situations. Practice your technique regularly, as this relatively simple technique has a multitude of uses.

USING THE ROLL CAST

When casting a fly, it is imperative that the line is straight at all times to ensure that tension is placed on the rod, and to avoid slack line developing, which can lead to the fly striking a part of your anatomy. The roll cast is the perfect answer to these problems, and is primarily used to straighten the line sharply before making an overhead cast (*see* pp.58–59). The roll cast is also ideal for casting in enclosed situations, as very little line passes behind the angler during its execution. Finally, a roll cast can be used as a safety technique to pull sinking lines to the surface prior to re-casting, which reduces the water tension placed on the line.

THE GRIP
Place your thumb on top of the cork handle and imagine that you are gently holding a screwdriver to achieve a comfortable, well-balanced grip. Ensure that your grip is relaxed at all times.

1 **Begin with the tip** of the rod low to the water and two rod-lengths of fly line on the water's surface, your elbow tucked in to your side, and your arm relaxed. Imagine a clock face at your side with your rod as the hour hand and 12 o'clock above your head. This sequence shows a right-handed cast; if you are left-handed, alter the "times" accordingly—for example, 11 o'clock will be 1 o'clock.

2 **Raise the rod tip** smoothly to 11 o'clock, using your elbow, not your wrist. This action will gradually peel the line from the water so that it slides across the surface in readiness for the back-cast.

3 **Tip your arm** slightly away from your body and slowly move the rod back to 1 o'clock. The fly line should fall behind the rod, creating a distinct "D" shape. Check that your thumb is almost upright and located in your peripheral vision. Make sure that a short section of line remains in the water, prior to starting the forward cast.

4 **From the one o'clock** position, smoothly accelerate the rod forward, following the direction of the line. Note the bend in the rod created by the line dragging against the water, a process known as "loading the rod."

5 **Stop the rod's** forward movement abruptly between 11 and 10 o'clock. Watch the line creating a narrow sausage shape as it extends, known as a casting loop.

Overhead casting

The overhead cast is the most common of all fly casts, and is most effective when used with the roll cast. It is not a difficult technique to grasp, but requires a little hand–eye coordination and timing. Practice overhead casts in a safe, wide-open space such as a playing field.

USING THE OVERHEAD CAST

Although the overhead cast does not have as many uses as the roll cast, it is an essential fly-fishing skill. The technique eliminates the pressure placed on the line by the water, and this results in substantial line speed and, consequently, a "loaded" rod (*see* step 4). Once unloaded,

the line achieves distances unobtainable with a roll cast. If fishing with a dry fly, use the overhead cast to pass air through the feathers to aid buoyancy. The overhead cast can also be used in most stillwater fly-fishing situations. It involves an extension of line behind the angler, so is unsuitable for enclosed environments.

1 Start off with your rod low to the water's surface, as for the roll cast. Keep your grip on the rod relaxed and your arm relaxed and tucked into your side. Imagine the clock face once again.
This sequence shows and describes a right-handed cast; if you are casting with your left hand, alter the "times" accordingly—for example, 11 o'clock will be 1 o'clock and vice versa.

2 Smoothly raise the rod tip to 11 o'clock, using your elbow, not your wrist. This will gradually peel the line from the water and create a bend in the rod, in readiness for the back-cast.

3 Bring the rod back, accelerating smoothly, until your thumb is adjacent to your eye with its nail in a near-vertical position and the rod tip at 1 o'clock. To create the right amount of speed, imagine you are gently flicking mud from the rod tip. Ensure that the rod remains motionless once the movement has been completed, to allow a loop to form.

4 As the line extends behind you, pause while saying "WAIT" or "TICK," which permits the loop to completely unroll and place tension on the rod. This process is known as "loading," and is critical to a successful cast. If you do not pause, slack line will create an audible "crack," which can break the leader.

5 Accelerate the rod forward, ensuring that your elbow stays tucked at your side. Look straight ahead. Do not look into the sky or down to the ground as this will create a casting angle that makes it difficult to land the fly line gently in the water at the end of the cast.

6 Bring the rod to a halt between 11 and 10 o'clock, saying "PUSH" or "TOCK." The line will pass over the tip of the rod, forming a loop. Ensure that the upper part of the loop passes close to the lower part, as this will create a tight, wind-resistant loop.

7 Allow the fly line to straighten out above the water as the rod gently falls back to the start position. Aim to land the fly line gently on the surface with as little disturbance to the water as possible.

Double-hauling

The double-haul is not so much a cast in its own right, but rather a series of coordinated hand movements applied to the overhead cast to create more tension within the rod. A well-executed double-haul will attain optimum line speeds and help achieve a tight, aerodynamic loop.

USING THE DOUBLE-HAUL

The double-haul technique should be used when you are fishing with flies at long range, to help you achieve maximum distance with minimal effort. Large, artificial patterns have a great deal of air-resistance and may be heavy—casting them with the double-haul combats both

these problems because the line effectively slices through the air. The double-haul is also highly effective in windy conditions. Furthermore, it can be used to present the fly accurately, as the rapidly moving line is more likely to reach its target. Only attempt double-hauling once you are proficient at overhead casting.

1 **Assume the low rod** position and relaxed grip that is used for roll and overhead casting. Take the fly line in your free hand, which is known as the line-control hand. Your two hands should be 4–12 in (10–30 cm) apart. Begin the back-cast, ensuring that you do not release your grip on the line with your line-control hand until required in the forward-cast phase of the sequence.

2 **As the rod accelerates** backward, make a short, smooth pull downward with your line-control hand. Imagine bouncing a ball on the ground as you make this movement, and say "HAUL" as you do so.

3 **Allow the line-control hand** to begin moving toward its original starting position as the line extends fully into the back-cast. Say "FEED" during this movement and ensure that you make it smooth and unhurried.

DOUBLE-HAULING IN SALTWATER

Use the double-haul on tropical saltwater flats to shoot rapid, accurate presentations to species such as bonefish and permit. It greatly increases your chances of catching these nervous fish, and is effective for casting the heavy crab and shrimp patterns often required. It is also handy when fly-fishing for fast-moving species, such as bass, that require baitfish patterns to be constantly strip-retrieved.

HIGH-SPEED DOUBLE-HAUL
Incorporating a double-haul into an overhead cast will cause the line to blur at high speed toward its target. This is a particularly useful technique for fly-fishing on tropical saltwater flats.

4 Pause, allowing the line to extend behind you while your line-control hand returns to its original starting position, ready for the next stage.

5 Begin the forward-cast with your rod hand, while also hauling with the line-control hand as you did in step 2, and saying "HAUL."

6 As you complete the forward-cast, say "FEED" and release the line, or repeat the steps to extend the line and achieve more distance.

Striking, playing, and landing fish

When a fish has finally taken your lure, fly, or bait, you need to
know just when to strike to set the hook, and how to fight or play it.
This is not an exact science—your instinct will always be important.
Landing fish follows basic rules that apply to most species.

WHEN TO STRIKE

Sometimes the fish will hit your lure, fly,
or bait so hard that it ends up hooking
itself. Lifting the rod into the fighting fish
will then keep the line straight so the
hook does not work loose and fall out.
But some species fiddle around with baits
for a while before taking them properly,
so you need to understand when to
strike, sweeping the rod back or sideways
to set the hook in the fish's mouth.

While you are watching for a visual
sign of a bite, such as a float dipping,
a dry fly being taken, or your rod tip
bouncing, try to gauge when to strike
by what you can feel through the line
and rod. Have patience, and wait until
the fish has picked up the bait, or taken
the fly properly. Some fish have hard
mouths and require that you strike hard
and repeatedly, but for most species, you
need not make exaggerated movements.

PLAYING A FISH

When a fish is small, it can be wound in
without playing. For larger fish, the drag
on your reel should be set so that the fish
can take line when it runs, with just

A RAPID STRIKE
The fish has taken the fly so fast that there is still
loose line to clear as the angler strikes and sets
the hook. Keep clear of loose line as the fish runs.

enough resistance to tire the fish without
risking a broken line. You will lose fewer
fish with a tight line. While you are
playing a fish, use one hand to hold the
foregrip of the rod, and the other to turn
the reel handle.

KEEPING THE LINE TIGHT
The rod is not working against the fish unless there
is bend in it, and the more strain you can put on the
fish, the sooner it will tire.

LANDING YOUR CATCH

As you play the fish, you will begin to feel it tire. The runs and lunges may become shorter and less powerful, or the fish may come to the surface and be easier to pull in. Landing techniques vary; some fish are easily captured in a landing net, while others are too large and powerful for this. If you can, netting is always the safest way to land a fish.

Other methods include lifting it out with the rod; pulling the line up, and grabbing the fish by the tail or another accessible part (only take hold of the mouth if you know the fish does not have sharp teeth); unhooking it in the water with a disgorger or T-bar; or beaching it. To beach a fish on a seashore, let the waves wash it on to the beach until you can safely grab it. If you are on a river or lake, you may be able to steer a fish close to the edge of the water. When landing fish, watch the water conditions, and do not go out too far into the water and get into difficulties.

LANDING WITH TWO
For big, heavy fish, you need an extra pair of hands to net your catch. The angler can use two hands for the rod, while a companion wades in with the net.

TAILING

Play the fish out, and then carefully grab it by the "wrist" of the tail. The shape of the tail prevents the fish from slipping out of your hand. Some species, such as trevally, have a sharp ridge on the tail wrist, so be sure to wear protective gloves to tail them. You need to be close to or in the water to tail a fish; be sure to play it safe.

Unhooking and releasing fish

Check whether local regulations permit catch-and-release. If you can return fish to the water, you need to unhook them, care for them, and release them in a way that ensures full recovery. If you intend to catch fish to eat, you must know how to despatch them quickly and humanely.

UNHOOKING A FISH

It may be possible to take the hook out with your fingers, especially when using a small, barbless hook. For fish with teeth, or when the hook is deeper inside the mouth, use a special tool, such as long-nosed pliers, a disgorger, or a T-bar. Keep the fish's time out of the water to a minimum, unhooking it either in, or very close to, the water. Wear protective gloves when unhooking a fish with sharp teeth, or a big, powerful fish, for it may move suddenly while you are unhooking. If a big fish, like a shark, has taken a bait down farther than its mouth, cut the wire trace as close to the hook-eye as possible; the acidic stomach juices of the shark, plus the saltwater, will soon rust the hook out. Make sure that the fish is fully supported when you unhook it, to prevent distress; big freshwater fish like carp should be laid out on a wetted mat.

UNHOOKING SAFELY
Removing a hook is often easier with one person to hold the fish and one to remove the hook. A tool that holds the fish firmly, but safely, by the chin can help.

CARING FOR FISH

A fish will be tired after a fight. Unless it is dispatched quickly for eating, you need to take care of the fish to enable it to recover. Many fish that have come in quickly can be unhooked and released immediately because they have expended little energy. But if a fish has fought hard, or has been hooked deeper than the mouth, take time to revive it.

Cradle the fish to support its weight in the water, face into any current to allow well-oxygenated water to run through the gills, and allow the fish to regain its strength while in your hands. If it is big, consider holding it by the tail either over the side of the boat or by wading out in the water with the fish held as best you can.

STAY CLOSE TO WATER
Most people value a photograph of their hard-won catch. Remove the fish from the water for as short a time as possible. Hold the fish close to the water for the photograph, cradling it gently to support its weight while it is out of the water.

RELEASING FISH

As soon as a fish is strong enough to swim away with enough energy to survive, it is time to release it. If you take time to revive a fish that has fought hard, you will feel when it is ready to be released. When the fish starts to kick hard, and tries to swim away, remove your hands and allow it to move off. Watch as it swims away, in case you need to grab it and help it for a while longer. Fish caught in deep water and affected by pressure change, such as cod, should be humanely dispatched as quickly as possible. These fish are badly affected by rapid changes in depth, and their swim bladders distend so much that they are unable to swim back down. Really large fish like sharks and marlin are released at the side of the boat.

HOLDING INTO THE CURRENT

In a river you can help your fish to revive by holding it so that the running water flows over its gills. This fish is in perfect condition and has fully recovered.

WEIGHING FISH

Most anglers want to know how much their fish weighs, and there are different types of weighing scales and slings to safely hold the fish while you weigh it. A tool, such as a Boga-Grip, that safely grips the chin of the fish for landing and unhooking, also has a built-in weighing scale that allows you to weigh it at the same time. The main thing is to weigh a fish without causing any extra distress. With experience, you will probably learn to estimate the weight of fish fairly accurately.

Using a
Boga-Grip

Bait- and lure-fishing

Bait- and lure-fishing provide a variety of opportunities for the adventurous angler. You will find that much of what you learn in freshwater with baits and artificial lures is also applicable to saltwater, and to fly-fishing. Starting with baits and lures is a logical way of approaching many types of water and species. Using the strategies in this chapter, you will be able to put your new skills into practice.

Lake-fishing for carp

Fishing for big carp on large expanses of water is an increasingly popular form of angling. Special lakes exist throughout Europe, and with large numbers of big wild carp in North America, anglers in the USA and Canada are starting to take notice of this prized fish.

RIG SETUP

In well-fished waters, the carp become wise to certain baits and rigs over time. To keep pace with this, big technological advances have taken place within carp fishing. The usual rig is a bottom-fishing set-up with a hair-rig arrangement (*below*). Weight, line, and trace are in camouflage coloring, so that these wary fish are not spooked. The weighted line sits on the bottom.

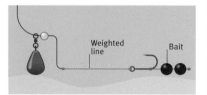

Weighted line

Bait

HAIR RIG
The bait is attached to the hook on a fine line. The fish sucks up the bait without feeling the hook.

BIG-PIT REEL
Large spinning reels for carp fishing (known as big-pit reels) come with high-capacity, wide spools that make it easier for you to load the line evenly. The more smoothly line comes off the reel during a cast, the farther the baited rig will fly.

SETTING UP AND PREPARING YOUR SWIM

Carp anglers spend long periods on the water and therefore need equipment to remain comfortable—this may include a shelter for night-fishing, a bed, a sleeping bag, and thermal clothing for cold weather. It is common to set up at least three rods, to enable you to cover as much water as possible.

Carp prefer to feed near some form of cover, so look to place your baits near islands, reed beds, visible sand bars, sunken trees, and drop-offs. Many lakes have favored swims (fishing areas) where carp are caught frequently. Throw or catapult groundbait into your chosen swim, to encourage the carp to come into the area. Cast your rig into this area, and carp may pick it up while feeding. A hooked carp often runs for cover, hence the need for a large reel, strong mainline, and a powerful, through-action carp rod that absorbs shocks and provides power to turn fish away from snags.

1 **Spend time looking** for signs of fish before setting up. Keep an eye out for carp rolling on the surface, reeds moving around because carp are knocking them, and water visibly stirred up by carp feeding in the shallows.

2 **Secure extra groundbait** to your rig, in a PVA net bag, held in place by foam, before casting. The bag dissolves quickly, to leave your baited rig surrounded by tempting morsels.

3 **Cast accurately** to where your groundbait lies, using a simple overhead cast, and looking up at the sky at about 45 degrees when releasing. Carp rods have a forgiving through action that enables smooth long-range casting.

4 **Place each rod** on a rod rest and into an electronic bite alarm. This will produce sounds and light indicators on the receiver when a fish picks up your bait.

STOPPING THE REEL
Spinning reels require require the angler to use an index finger to secure the line during the cast. Release the line at the end of the cast.

5 **Watch patiently for a bite.** Fishing for big carp is all about putting in the time. Some waters may produce few fish, but the longer your baits are fishing in the right areas, the greater your chances of hooking a monster carp.

Tent

Bite-alarm indicator

Baits

Multiple rods on rod rest with bite alarms

Carp bed on which to place your catch

Stalking for carp

Seeking out feeding carp and then perhaps entering the water to fish for them is an exciting way to target these large freshwater fish. Any kind of sight-fishing, which involves seeing the fish you are hoping to catch, adds an extra edge to your enjoyment of the sport.

ROD AND RIG SETUP

A standard 12-ft (3.7-m) carp rod is a good choice, but many anglers prefer shorter stalking rods for fishing in confined areas. Mono line has a degree of stretch for safety when hooking fish at close range, but it sinks, whereas braid is sensitive and floats, which is useful for surface fishing. Travel light; the more mobile you are, the closer you'll be able to get to the fish.

SPINNING REEL
A large capacity spinning reel copes well with stalking. It is worth carrying a smaller, lighter reel if you do a lot of mobile sight-fishing.

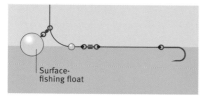

Surface-fishing float

SURFACE RIG
A float such as a carp controller will enable you to cast to the fish. If they are close, you may be able to freeline bait.

FINDING AND FISHING FOR CARP

Stalking for carp is all about finding the fish, which is best done by walking and looking. Move stealthily and do not let the fish see you first. Dawn and dusk are good times of day to spot them. The quieter the water, the greater the chance of sight-fishing; fish shy away from noise and vibrations.

Carp suck bait rather than charge in and engulf it, so hesitate for a split second before striking when you see a fish take your bait. Initially, watch them feeding to learn their habits, and build up their confidence before introducing baited hooks into the area.

1 Find an elevated vantage point from which to look for fish—even carefully climbing a sturdy tree, if necessary. Wear polarized sunglasses to cut glare and enable you to see into the water. In order not to spook the fish, dress in dull-colored clothing, remain quiet, and do not break natural horizons.

2 **Pre-bait your chosen spots**
with groundbait of bread
or dog biscuits, and regularly
check these areas. If the carp
come up for the groundbait,
use it for hookbait too.
Lightweight chest waders
are useful. Step carefully
and do not go out too deep.

3 **Keep as still as possible** when carp
are feeding very close to you. It can
get exciting, but you must be stealthy.
Fish are naturally wary of foreign objects
in the water and on the bank, and their
eyesight is very acute, so once in position,
make sure you make as little disturbance
as possible when moving. Carry some
bait with you so that there is no need
to leave the water to rebait the hook.

4 **Land your carp** with a large, soft-
mesh landing net, and unhook
and weigh it on a wetted carp mat
or in a sling that will not damage the
natural protective slime. Keep the
fish near the water and make sure
its time out is short to reduce stress.

Fishing for pike

Pike fishing is popular in many parts of the world. These hard-fighting predators can be caught on both baits and lures, and they provide one of the ultimate freshwater challenges—taking them using light-tackle lure-fishing techniques is incredibly exciting.

ROD AND RIG SETUP

Small lure rods enable you to fish for long periods. They have plenty of power to deal with large pike, but find out what size fish you might encounter and tailor your tackle accordingly. Longer, heavier pike rods, better suited to bait-fishing, can work for lures, although from a boat it is best to use a spinning or casting rod under 10 ft (3 m) in length and rated to cast the lure weights you will be using. As for reels, it's a matter of whether you prefer a small baitcasting reel or a small to medium spinning reel.

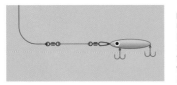

PIKE-FISHING RIG
Use braid line and a wire biting trace. Mono will not withstand a pike's teeth. Many fishing waters demand the use of barbless hooks.

SUBSURFACE LURE
Pike respond to lures at all depths and in various designs, from a wobbling type of shallow diver to a heavy jerkbait.

PREPARING FOR PIKE

The real trick to catching pike is to find the kind of habitat that they like to lurk around and feed in. An electronic fish finder can also be useful in locating them. As well as showing the fish, it reveals the configuration of the bottom, allowing you to identify fish-holding features such as underwater islands, lumps of rock, sunken trees, and holes. Begin by fishing your lures in and around these sites as well as close to the bank, particularly where there are large reed beds or overhanging or dead trees.

Carry a selection of lures to cover a range of depths, from tight to the bottom to on the surface. There is a good chance that your lure will pass close to the pike many times before they decide to hit it, so work the water systematically. Move quietly around the boat, as sound carries through water and may spook the fish.

A big landing net is essential, as is a glove for protecting your hands when unhooking. Many anglers like to unhook pike on a wetted carp mat on the bottom of the boat, but it is often possible to safely remove the hooks from the fish in the net at the side of the boat.

1 When casting from your boat, adopt a steady stance, for movement is always exaggerated when a boat is rocking slightly. Anchoring will allow you to place the boat to give maximum lure coverage, but if the wind is light, consider slowly drifting through the area.

2 **Takes can be savage**. The pike often engulfs the lure before you register that you need to strike. Maintain a bend in the rod during the fight and, as far as possible, keep the fish's head toward you to prevent it from reaching sanctuary.

3 **Position the net** just below the water surface. As the pike tires, draw it over the net's mouth and lift the net. It is possible to "glove" a pike (grab it at the bottom of the gills where it is bony and will not be damaged) for unhooking, but this requires experience.

4 **Hold the pike** by the bony part of the lower gill area and unhook using long-nosed pliers or a special unhooking implement. Wear a glove and do not put your fingers near the fish's jaws. A pike's teeth are numerous and sharp and are designed to grab prey and not let go.

USING FISH BAIT

Baits are an excellent way to catch pike, using long, powerful rods that enable you to cast heavy weights. Bottom-fished dead baits work well close to structures, and are often fished carp-style with bait alarms, but one of the most enjoyable methods is to fish dead and livebaits under floats (check local regulations on livebaits). Use a fairly large, buoyant float to support the bait at the required depth, and use a wire trace. Make the most of the current on a river, or the breeze on a lake, to steer your float, and keep an eye on its movements. Do not strike until the pike pulls the float under hard.

Lake-fishing for largemouth bass

Among both pleasure and competition anglers, the largemouth bass is one of the most popular freshwater species in the US. Many lakes in the southern US hold large numbers, and anglers usually fish for them from fast boats that have a shallow draft for access to all areas.

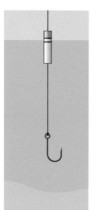

ROD AND RIG SETUP

Bass rods are usually short—which is preferable on a boat—and powerful to assist in setting the hook in the bass's bony mouth and for keeping these strong fish away from snags. Small baitcasting reels are the most popular reels, as they offer good control when fishing lures and baits in tight areas, but spinning reels also work well.

LARGEMOUTH BASS RIG
Use a simple float setup for fishing with livebaits. Lures can also be used for bass fishing. Braid mainlines are increasingly popular as they give direct, accurate fishing.

SMALL BAITCASTER
The demands of bass fishing have led to developments in small baitcasting multiplier reels, such as electronic braking systems.

HIGH-SPEED BOAT FISHING

Like many other species, largemouth bass thrive around areas of cover and shelter. Because their feeding habits vary according to atmospheric pressure and water temperature, boats are used to provide access to the ever-changing bass-holding areas. High-speed boats are popular because the faster you can travel, the more fishing time you will have. Special bass boats are usually equipped with big engines, fish finders, and livebait wells. Many have seats on the bow to sit on and cast from, and a separate, foot-controlled, electric motor for a quiet final approach to the fish.

1 **Accurate casting** is vital as the fish are often hidden, and fishing with either lures or livebaits requires precision. The more good ground you cover with a lure, the greater your chances of hooking up; the closer you cast livebait to a likely spot, the more likely a bass is to come out and hit it.

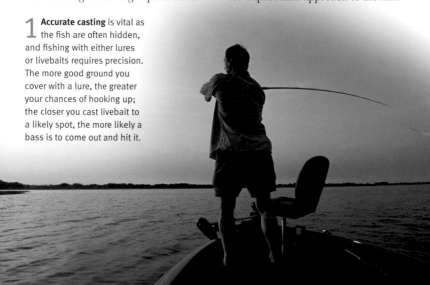

CHOOSING LURES

There are an enormous number of freshwater bass lures. Soft plastics are popular for fishing at all depths, and are cheap enough to replace if ripped up by the fish. All manner of hard plastic lures work well, including shallow-diving ones.

2 **Strike the fish** hard and start winding almost in one motion, particularly when you are close to an underwater structure. It is vital to turn the bass away from potential danger as quickly as possible, and then play it out in the clear water closer to the boat.

3 **Using a net** is the safest and most efficient way to land your catch. The easiest way to land the fish is to have the net's mouth under the water and bring the fish over it. The person with the net then scoops it up.

4 **Hold the fish** by its bottom jaw and be careful not to cause it any distress. Keep its time out of the water to an absolute minimum.

Pier fishing

Man-made structures often give easy and safe access to deeper water. Schools of small fish often gather around piers, breakwaters, and harbor walls, and bigger predators also congregate, attracted by this potential food source. Many people fish for their first time from a pier.

ROD AND RIG SETUP

One of the most effective ways to fish from a pier is to set up a simple float-fishing rig. Use a longer spinning or casting rod to aid with casting the float out, and match it with a medium spinning reel. A float that carries a weight of 1–2 oz (30–60 g) is perfect for casting and fishing. Be careful when casting to avoid injury to others on the pier.

Weight

BASIC FLOAT RIG
A baited hook suspended under a float allows you to target fish that are not feeding on the bottom.

SPINNING REEL
A spinning reel offers tangle-free casting and is perfect for float-fishing.

EXPLOITING MAN-MADE STRUCTURES

Piers often attract large numbers of fish taking advantage of the feeding opportunities offered by species that make their homes in the structure, such as crabs and crustaceans. Small fish often gather in the shelter of piers and harbor walls. Some piers offer exciting fishing for large species—for example, tarpon fishing from the piers of southern Florida. Be sure to check that fishing is allowed from the pier you intend to go to.

1 **Choose your baits and equipment** to suit the waters and the likely targets. You may need a drop net to land big fish if the distance down to the water is too great for a traditional landing net.

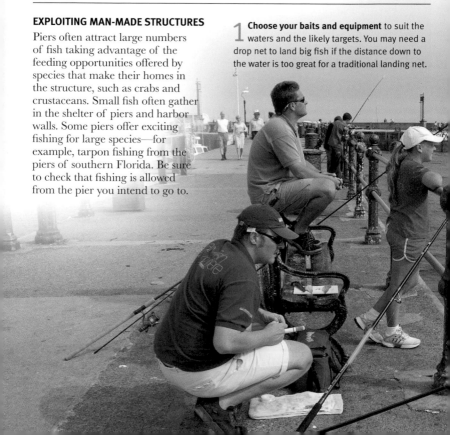

2 **Concentrate hard** on watching all movements of the float, and strike when it goes under the surface. The float is the bite indicator in float-fishing. When it suddenly goes under the surface or starts moving erratically, there is a fish eating the bait.

3 **When you have a bite**, strike and reel in. Different fish will swim at different depths, so set up the rig accordingly. For example, to hook mackerel the bait needs to be set about 6 ft (2 m) under the float.

Fishing for striped bass

Among the most popular and important saltwater species in the US, striped bass, or "stripers," are migratory fish. The best places to fish for them have prime times of year when the most or biggest fish can be caught, from boats or the shore, using baits, lures, or flies.

ROD AND RIG SETUP

A short spinning or casting rod of 8 ft (2.4 m) is perfect for boat-fishing for stripers, when using lures or bait (live and dead). Combine it with a spinning or conventional reel. Modern braid main-lines are a good choice because they provide such direct contact with the fish, and are much stronger than mono lines of similar width. However, it is important to adjust the drag (or clutch) on your reel to compensate for their lack of stretch. A #9 saltwater fly-fishing set-up works well. Carry floating and sinking lines.

BASIC FLOAT RIG
For fishing in a current and near underwater structures, use a basic float rig with a 50-lb (23-kg) mono leader and a sharp 6/o hook.

SPINNING REEL
A spinning reel is ideal for drifting drifting baits under a float. You can use the secondary drag system to pay out your line and then simply turn the handle to engage the reel ready for the strike. However, many anglers prefer to open the bale arm to feed out the line.

BOAT-FISHING FOR STRIPED BASS

Like many saltwater fish, stripers use cover to hunt and feed around, and many boat-anglers use the wind and currents to push their baits and lures close to likely fish-holding areas. A favored method in many areas is to steer or anchor the boat precisely so that your float-fished cut bait (cut-up fish) works its way back toward an underwater structure, such as shallow, rocky ground, or perhaps a bridge or pier. It is also exciting to ease boats close to the structure and cast into the best-looking spots. Take up a stable and comfortable casting position and cover as much water as possible.

To maneuver close to a structure, you must be very capable of handling a boat in this kind of situation, or have an extremely knowledgeable skipper. Never take a boat anywhere near a rocky shore if you lack experience. Watch out at all times for other water traffic and keep an eye on the state of the sea and weather. Remember that tides rise and fall, sometimes quite significantly.

1 **Start to introduce** chunks of baitfish (mackerel works well) into the tide, once the boat is anchored, so that they drift toward the fish-holding areas. As with freshwater groundbaiting, little and often is the key; you want the fish to be interested, but not full. Place a chunk on your hook, set the float, and use the tide or current to drift the bait back toward the structure.

2 **Watch the float,** not only for a bite, but also for where it goes with the tide. Pay out enough line to let it float naturally, but keep it tight enough to strike. When it is in a likely fish-holding spot, it is worth holding the float back for a short while.

3 **When you hook a striper,** play it out from the structure as hard as you can—it will try to find sanctuary. On a boat, the easiest way to land a fish is by using a net, especially when the water is choppy. Landing nets with large openings make it comparatively straightforward to steer the fish in and over the net so that your companion can scoop it up.

SHORE-FISHING FOR STRIPED BASS

Much striped-bass fishing is done from rocks, beaches, and piers or in estuaries, as migrating stripers come close to shore to feed and spawn; the big females, or cows, are a saltwater angler's dream. These conditions present a great opportunity for fishing with flies, lures, or baits.

Many of the biggest stripers are caught at night from quiet rock marks, often in rough conditions. Beaches and estuaries usually offer easier access for good fishing. If you find schools of herring feeding close in, there is a good chance that stripers will be feeding on them, so keep your eyes open and look out for signs of fish moving around.

STRIPED BASS CAUGHT ON THE FLY
When fly-fishing for stripers, use a line tray for stripping line into, so that the movement of the sea does not take your spare line away from you.

Small-boat inshore fishing

Small boats allow anglers to fish in waters that might be inaccessible to larger boats. Those that have a shallow draft can be used in shallow water and confined spaces. For ultra-shallow waters in tropical seas, there are special flats boats.

ROD AND RIG SETUP

Most anglers who fish from boats carry a variety of rods and reels. They must be stowed carefully to avoid damage as you move around the boat. It is useful to have short, powerful spinning or casting rod that is suitable for spinning, jigging, float- and bottom-fishing.

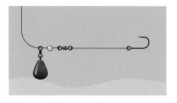

BOTTOM-FISHING RIG
The diagram shows a typical bottom-fishing rig employed for this type of fishing. Use a wire trace for fish with sharp teeth.

ROUND BAITCASTING REEL
When filled with braid, a round baitcasting reel is a good all-around boat reel. Surprisingly large fish can be landed on this type of baitcasting reel.

WARM-CLIMATE SMALL-BOAT FISHING

In warm waters there are plenty of species that feed either close to or right at the surface. Many areas close to shore hold good stocks of fish, and a small boat may be the only way of accessing them. Channels, flats, and mangrove areas, for instance, may be accessible only in a boat, and yield species such as snook, tarpon, snappers, and bonefish.

As you cruise around in the boat, keep an eye open for signs of fish activity. For example, a school of jacks voraciously feeding on bait on the surface or flocks of birds diving may indicate that there are predatory fish swimming below. The faster you can get close to such an area, the greater your chances of success. It is worth always having a lure-fishing rod set up with a surface popper (*see* p.40) to cast into an area of this type of fish activity.

SAFETY CONSIDERATIONS

Wherever you choose to fish, take the right safety equipment: lifejackets for everybody, plus a VHF radio and distress flares. Do not rely on cell phones for your safety. Anyone who is to be in control of a boat should have attended an appropriate course beforehand.

1 **Feel for a bite** by holding the line between thumb and index finger. This helps to stabilize the rod and is a perfect position for a quick strike. Short rods work well when the butt is under your armpit, but try different positions to find what is best for you.

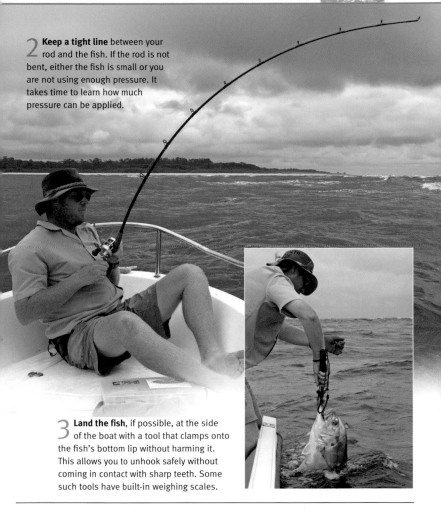

2 **Keep a tight line** between your rod and the fish. If the rod is not bent, either the fish is small or you are not using enough pressure. It takes time to learn how much pressure can be applied.

3 **Land the fish**, if possible, at the side of the boat with a tool that clamps onto the fish's bottom lip without harming it. This allows you to unhook safely without coming in contact with sharp teeth. Some such tools have built-in weighing scales.

COLD-CLIMATE SMALL-BOAT FISHING

Many species in cold waters like to feed closer to the bottom, if not actually on it. Your tackle choices need to reflect this: the heavier the weight required to hold the rig on the bottom or to sink your lures and baits down deep, the more powerful your rod must be.

Always be aware of the local weather forecasts and listen to updates on your boat's radio. While fog can be worrying when out at sea, your GPS and radar will help you to get home safely. When traveling in fog, always show appropriate lights. It is vital to make sure somebody on board keeps watch for other vessels at all times. Be sure to give a wide berth to those that show up on your radar.

DRESSED FOR COLD SEAS
A flotation suit has a built-in closed-cell foam lining that will help to float if you fall in, and it keeps you warm, which will help you to fish more effectively. A flotation suit is not a substitute for a lifejacket.

Slow trolling for salmon

Chinook and coho are among the salmon species that school in the Pacific Ocean to feed prior to returning to rivers to spawn. This is when many anglers use trolling methods for them at sea. Whether close to shore or miles from land, the methods used are similar.

ROD AND RIG SETUP

A downrigger uses a wire line and heavy weight to hold lures down deep. This means you do not have a weight on your rod, which gives a different feel when you fight the fish. Use soft-tipped rods, as they bend over easily when the line is clipped to the downrigger. Braided mainlines are advised.

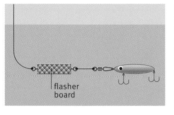

SALMON RIG SETUP
A lure is usually fished behind a reflective "flasher board." This is a plastic board that spins enticingly when it is trolled at the correct speed. The board's movement attracts the salmon, which then see your lure just beyond.

CONVENTIONAL REEL
Conventional reels are popular for trolling, as are "mooching" reels. Similar to centerpins, the latter do not have a drag system or gears. The handle revolves when a fish takes the line.

HOW A DOWNRIGGER WORKS

A downrigger is an electronic or mechanical winching device that keeps lures at a set depth (usually fairly deep) when trolling. It does this by means of a thin, strong wire line with a heavy weight at the end. Just above the weight is a special line clip to which your rig is attached; rig and weight are then lowered via the downrigger. Your mainline is held in place by the clip until a fish hits your lure. The heavy weight and thin wire cut through the water as they are slowly trolled behind the boat.

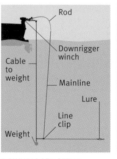

DOWNRIGGER SETUP
The mainline from the rod is threaded though the line clip on the weighted downrigger wire, to secure the rig at the required depth. As soon as a fish takes the lure, the clip releases the line, and the rod tip springs forward.

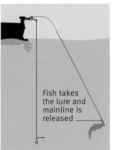

DOWNRIGGER IN ACTION
Most boats use at least two downriggers, many of which are electronically controlled. Linked into the boat's power system, they will do all the winding in of the heavy weight for you. Downriggers have a long arm that sticks out from the side of the boat, which helps to prevent the lures from tangling. Use the fish-finder and the downrigger's depth counter to fish the correct depths without snagging.

TROLLING IN ACTION

Trolling for salmon is generally done at a slow, constant speed, often with a small engine. Once the lures are set on the downriggers, steer the boat through fish-holding areas. Chinook and coho can put up a dogged fight, especially the large chinook, which is often caught when trolling near the bottom. Stock levels of these fish are monitored and the numbers that anglers can keep are tightly controlled. This protects salmon stocks, ensuring that plenty of fish can get back into the rivers to spawn.

DOWNRIGGER TECHNIQUES

Clip your line into the line clip on the downrigger and put your reel in free-spool mode (remember to control it). Let the downrigger drop the weight down, controlling your reel as your lure descends. Stop the weight at your chosen depth, click your reel into gear, and wind your line down tight to the clip. Set your drag for when a fish hits, and then place your rod into its holder.

1 **When a fish bites,** your rod tip suddenly springs back because the clip has freed your line. Grab the rod and wind down hard on the reel right until you can feel the kicking fish. Salmon can fight powerfully and aggressively in the open sea. The soft-tipped rod helps to protect your hook-hold by absorbing the fish's lunges.

2 **Land your fish** with the help of a landing net, and remove the hook with care. Coho salmon are superb fish and one of the most prized of Pacific salmon species. Respect the rules regarding the number of fish you can keep, and return as many as possible to the water.

Bait-fishing for tarpon

Tarpon are among the most impressive and hard-fighting fish in the world, famous for their awesome speed, power, and acrobatic jumps, as well as their ability to throw hooks. They grow very large and represent a great challenge on any kind of rig.

TARPON RIG
Use a float, a sharp 6/0 or 7/0 hook, and a short length of 100-lb (45-kg) biting (or "rubbing") leader.

ROD AND RIG SETUP

Short, powerful rods are used for bait-fishing; for tarpon they are often heavy-rated spinning or casting rods that have sufficient strength to cope with this extreme sport. Many anglers prefer mono lines of around 30-lb (13.5-kg) breaking strain—the inherent stretch of this type of line can help to cushion the impact of the tarpon's runs and jumps. But increasingly, heavy braid mainlines are used, which offer a greater strength-to-diameter ratio than mono. Anglers using such tackle are playing the tarpon as hard as possible, but nevertheless this fish will often still get away.

CONVENTIONAL REEL
Strong, modern conventional or spinning reels work equally well for this type of fishing. An effective drag system that will help you tire this powerful fish is also essential.

CHOOSING YOUR LOCATION

The Florida Keys are perfect for fishing tarpon—during their migration they are found here feeding on a mass of baitfish. They feed more readily in low light—dawn or dusk, or at night—and many anglers and guides are well practiced at hunting them during complete darkness. At other times, the numerous road bridges cast shadow in the water, offering the tarpon the cover or darker light they prefer. The deeper the water under the bridge, the greater your chances during daylight hours. Position the boat at anchor so that the tide will take your float-fished (or free-lined) baits back to where the tarpon are holding up.

There is no mistaking a tarpon bite—the float disappears and/or your line suddenly tightens up and pulls violently away. For this reason, it is vital that everybody on board knows exactly what to do the moment a fish is hooked—this is high-adrenaline fishing.

1 **Fish in the shadows** and deeper water beneath a bridge where tarpon are feeding during the daytime. They will be staying within the shadow lines. You will often see their big shapes on your fishfinder. Try to set your hook with repeated short strikes and then hold on. The fish will usually jump the moment it is hooked, and this is when it may manage to throw the hook. If the hook holds, be prepared for an awesome fight.

2 **Pursue the fish**. Your skipper will raise the anchor and head in the same direction as the fish. Get line back on the reel fast to fight on a short line—this gives more control when the fish charges off. "Bow to the fish" as the tarpon jumps out of the water, by lowering the rod tip to create slack line, which protects against the violent head-shaking of the fish.

HOOKING AND UNHOOKING TIPS

Tarpon are notorious for shedding hooks. Their hard, bony mouths are tricky to set a hook into, and their head-shaking tactics throw hooks too. Count on one fish per hook and use good-quality, chemically sharpened saltwater hooks. With J-hooks, strike repeatedly when the fish hits your bait; with circle hooks, let the fish tighten up against the reel. If you strike a circle hook, you will pull it straight out of the fish's mouth. Circle hooks are relatively easy to unhook and present no risk of being swallowed, which could cause damage to the fish.

3 **Landing a tarpon** is best done by grabbing the hard bottom lip while wearing gloves, and then unhooking. Tarpon are very carefully looked after and are rarely taken out of the water; most guides lean over, grab the fish, remove the hook, wait for a few photographs to be taken, and then release the fish.

Vertical jigging

Many anglers consider vertical jigging to be one of the most effective ways to use lures (or "jigs"). This technique is used for saltwater species, such as dogtooth tuna, California yellowtail, and big giant trevally, as well as freshwater fish, such as smallmouth bass and walleye.

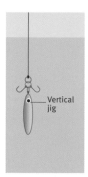

VERTICAL JIG RIG
Rig assist (or stinger) hooks above the jig using Kevlar cord and heavy-duty split rings.

ROD AND RIG SETUP

Jigging rods must be light and strong, to cope with continually working the sometimes heavy jigs in deep water, and then lifting big, powerful fish. These rods are about 7–8 ft (2–2.4 m) in length and rated to the lines or the weights of the jigs. Jigging requires the use of braided mainlines, which reduce stretch and drag in the water, and allow you to produce the required movement in the lure. Line with a high breaking strain can be used for strong fish, but always use a mono "rubbing" leader that resists abrasion and sharp teeth.

SPINNING REEL
Strong saltwater spinning reels are perfect for vertical jigging, but some anglers prefer conventional reels. Choose good quality—this fishing is hard on the equipment.

MODERN TECHNIQUES

Jigging is an old fishing technique that has been improved by modern methods and materials, as well as new technology. Light but powerful rods have helped anglers to land huge fish that would have previously required far heavier tackle. Electronic fish finders are used to locate the fish and allow you to place the jig near them. Special braided lines that change color along their length help you judge the exact depth of your jig.

Once the jig is in place, you need to make it come to life and appeal to the fish. There are many slightly different ways of working the jig, but the basic technique is to lift up the rod to lift the jig, and then lower the rod to allow it to flutter back down. Whether you reel in at the same time depends on where you are fishing and the species you are targeting. Vertical jigging is an active way of fishing—the longer your jig dances in fish-holding areas, the greater your chance of success. Vertical jigs are ideal for fast-moving predatory fish, but can be used to catch a variety of other species in warm and cold waters.

1 **Choose the size and weight** of jig to suit the waters you are fishing. Known as vertical or butterfly jigs, these lures are usually stored in wallets, which keep them separated and easy to identify. The jigs are designed to sink quickly and then flutter like a butterfly when worked with the right action on the correct rods and reels. Assist (or stinger) hooks help too.

MAINTAIN CONTACT
Braid mainlines enable
you to keep a very direct
contact to the lure.
Modern spinning reels
designed for saltwater
use are very robust and
will handle big fish
and tough fishing.

2 **Stand comfortably** and drop the jig to the desired depth. Now lift
(jerk) the rod as you turn the reel-handle upward, and drop the rod
as you turn the reel-handle downward. You can also jerk the rod up
without reeling. Do not make exaggerated rod movements.

3 **Set the drag** on your reel to match the
strength of the braid. This will enable
you to catch very big fish using vertical jigging
techniques. Use the power of the rod and braid
to lift hard into the fish, and then pump and
wind repeatedly to tire the fish and get line
back on the reel. Make sure you remain stable
and comfortable on the deck of the boat.

4 **Use a butt pad** when playing the fish,
in order to protect your groin and lower
stomach area from the butt of the rod. A butt
pad also provides a central pivot point that
enables you to apply pressure more effectively
to the fish. Deepwater reefs often produce
a wide range of large, colorful species of fish
that are attracted to vertical jigs.

Fly-fishing

The gentle art of fly-fishing is completely absorbing. From the most fundamental and traditional ways of presenting flies to fish, in both saltwater and freshwater, through to more modern approaches to the discipline of fly-fishing, these strategies will help you to catch all manner of fish species in a wonderful variety of waters. Casting artificial flies in rivers, lakes, and seas can be an intoxicating mix of the old and the new.

Reservoir and lake fly-fishing

Fly-fishing quietly from open boats is a wonderful way to fish, and in time the skills become second nature. When you take a boat out on a large lake or reservoir—having stowed your equipment—your main consideration is where the fish might be feeding.

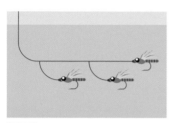

THE RIG
It can be very effective to use a team of flies (usually two or three) when fishing on a reservoir or lake. The point fly, which is the one farthest from the fly line, might be a heavy fly that helps the others sink a bit deeper.

ROD AND RIG SETUP
A 10-ft (3-m) #5 to #7 fly-fishing rod and matched reel will cover most fly-fishing situations on open water, such as reservoirs and lakes, including dry-fly fishing with floating lines, and nymph-fishing with intermediate or sinking lines. Most fly-anglers on boats use a large, top-opening boat-style tackle bag to hold their fly boxes, spare reels, lines, flies, leaders, and other tackle. It is always advisable to wear a lifejacket, and in some places it is mandatory.

BRIGHT LINE
You will find it easier to see a colored fly line. Attach a long, clear leader to avoid spooking the fish.

USING THE BOAT
Many lakes and reservoirs have fleets of small, open boats available to rent for fly-fishing. Often, conservation regulations permit only electric motors with 12V batteries, but speed is not important, and a quiet boat will spook fewer fish. Many anglers like to bring foldable seats for comfort during a long day on the water. Keep tackle bags close by you, to minimize movement on board.

When you are fishing in pairs, the least experienced angler should sit with a clear casting arc to his or her strongest side. If right-handed, he or she should sit farthest forward, facing out from the left-hand side of the boat; if left-handed, he or she should face the other way.

Tackle bags

Oars and
spare rods

Folding seat

Battery

Electric
motor

Landing
net

PACKING THE BOAT
Stow rods carefully where they cannot be stepped on, and store tackle neatly in bags or boxes. Leave as much clear space as possible for casting, playing, and landing fish.

Spare flies

FINDING THE FISH

Present dry flies and nymphs just below the surface where there are gentle ripples on top of the water, but fish may also be present in flat-calm stretches of water flanked by gentle ripples. In a small boat, always cast one at a time, and remain sitting down. The person casting must be sure to cast his line safely away from their fishing companion in the boat.

1 **Having cast a long line** to cover a large section of water with your fly, fish right back to the boat. Lift the fly gently from the water in case a fish is following it in.

2 **Maneuver the boat to explore** different fish-holding spots. In hot, still weather, look for fish around artificially oxygenated areas with bubbles on the surface. Features such as dam walls, overhanging trees, and other structures may also attract fish. Sit down to play the fish.

3 **Use a landing net** to bring your catch on board; keep the rod high, and draw the fish over the waiting net opening rather than chasing the fish with the net.

Fly-fishing on small rivers

Fly-fishing for trout and grayling in small rivers is one of the most delicate forms of angling. Tumbling water tends to have a hypnotic effect on the angler, and nobody tires of seeing these beautiful fish. Fishing for them requires light tactics and an expert touch.

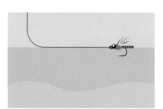

DRY-FLY RIG
A simple dry-fly rig works well for trout and grayling that are feeding on the surface. However, you can also use wet-fly tactics. Be sure to check the local regulations for what methods are allowed on the waters you are fishing.

ROD AND RIG SETUP

A light, 8-ft (2.4-m) #4 or #5 fly rod is usually suitable for fly-fishing in a river of this type. The rod should be matched with a small fly reel loaded with a floating line. Catching trout and grayling with dry flies as they rise to the surface to feed on insects is the classic way of taking them, but be prepared to fish with weighted nymphs (*see* Freshwater wet flies, p.44) if dry flies are not working. Tapered leaders no heavier than 4-lb (1.8-kg) breaking strain are adequate for most conditions.

SMALL-RIVER FLY REEL
A small, lightweight fly reel is perfectly suited to fishing small rivers. This reel holds enough line for most situations.

TARGETING TROUT AND GRAYLING

Look for these fish around landscape features and structures, whether overhanging branches, moving white water, sunken branches, or undercut banks. Fishing close to fast-moving water means that the fish are less likely to see you. Classic upstream dry-fly fishing, as described here, is perfect for delicate presentation to freely rising fish. However, as an alternative to a simple dry-fly rig, you could try a dry fly with a weighted nymph below—a useful way to fish simultaneously on the surface and along or near to the bottom. While accurate and delicate casting is an essential river-fishing technique, the ability to control how the river affects your fly and line is also vital, a technique termed "mending the line" (*see right*). Ideally, a dry fly should act naturally in the water; when you cast upstream, allow your fly to gently drift downstream in the current.

1 **After casting** and as your line starts to straighten after landing on the water, point your rod tip down the line and then delicately flip your arm and wrist upstream. This is called "mending the line" and is a way of allowing your fly to drift farther by adding some slack into the fly line, either during the cast, or when your fly line hits the water.

2 **Be prepared to change fly** if your initial choice is not working. Carry a selection of flies in their boxes in your fly-vest or jacket pocket, so that you can change flies while in the river. The less you move around, the less the fish will be spooked. Always be careful of your footing when wading in a river.

3 **Having landed your fish,** return it to the water. Hold it close to the surface of the water and gently slip it back in. Wild brown trout are pretty fish and, even if they might not be the largest fish you will catch, to take them from a small river is a true privilege.

CHECKING FOR LARVAE AND GRUBS

It can be extremely useful to scour around the river bottom, checking the types of indigenous grubs and larvae on which the fish in the particular waters you are fishing are feeding. This enables you to match your pattern of fly to the natural prey you find, which may increase your chance of a catch. Many landing nets have a finer net attached that can be spread out across the opening of the net and used to sift the river bottom.

Wet fly-fishing on lakes

Novice fly-anglers are well-advised to start fly-fishing with wet flies on small bodies of still water; larger lakes and reservoirs can be daunting for a newcomer to the sport. Well-stocked commercial fisheries tend to be easiest to fish. Rainbow trout are a common target.

ROD AND RIG SETUP

A #7 fly rod and reel suit this type of wet fly-fishing perfectly. You should either carry two reels, or use one with an interchangeable cartridge, because you will need to carry a floating and an intermediate or sinking line, for a variety of situations. Your range of wet flies should include a variety of patterns (*see* pp.44). Big lure patterns may attract trout, but carry some dry flies as well.

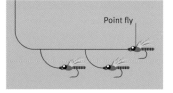

Point fly

TEAM OF FLIES
Fishing a team of flies allows you to set them up in different ways. Try a weighted wet fly as the point fly, to help sink the others deeper.

DAMSEL NYMPH MEDIUM (OLIVE)
Excellent for use if trout are rejecting bigger, brighter imitations, the Damsel Nymph Medium should be used with intermediate or floating fly lines, with varied retrieves.

STILLWATER FISHING

When considering where to cast, look for fish-holding areas such as natural bays, small streams coming into the lake, and vegetation at the water's edge. Watch for birds feasting on hatching insects; fish might also be feeding in these areas as the larvae head to the surface. Look for fish taking flies off the surface, or water movement as fish cruise around. Don't forget to talk to local anglers and the people who run the fisheries, as nothing beats local advice on fly patterns, fish movements, and water conditions.

1 **Use a smooth overhead cast** to put your flies out on the water. A team of flies is prone to tangling, so cast gently. Start with floating line, suitable for both wet and dry flies; in high sun, or cold weather, change to intermediate or fast-sinking line to take wet flies down deeper.

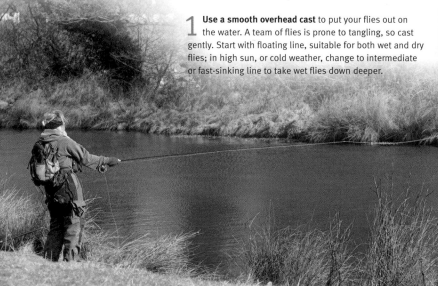

2 Cast and retrieve continually to give flies maximum time in the water. Making a figure-eight movement as you retrieve creates extra fly movement. Finally, consider tying on a single, garish lure pattern, then cast and retrieve quickly on floating and intermediate lines.

3 Keep your line tight once a fish is hooked. Keep a good bend in the rod, and use it to steer the fish over the waiting net, until it can be scooped up. Do not chase the fish with the net. If on your own, extend the net with one hand, and bring the fish over the net with the other.

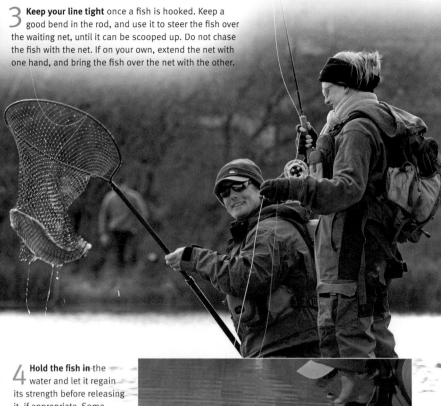

4 Hold the fish in the water and let it regain its strength before releasing it, if appropriate. Some fisheries are "put and take" only, where the fish you catch must be quickly and efficiently dispatched, to then take home and eat. The fishery records the numbers of fish taken, and frequently restocks.

Czech nymphing

Czech nymphing is an extremely effective method of fly-fishing in which a team of weighted flies is fished close to the bottom of the river. No long casting is required, but the delicate presentation is a skill that takes time to master.

ROD AND RIG SETUP

Equip yourself with a 10-ft (3-m) #5 to #7 fly rod, which gives a high degree of control when working a team of flies. Use a fly reel to match, and load it with a floating line. Make a leader no more than 6 ft (1.8 m) in length. A strike indicator can help keep the flies at the right depth, and also acts as a visual bite detector.

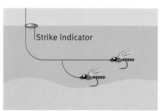

TEAM OF FLIES
The point fly is the lightest of the team of flies, designed to rise slightly in the water; tie on one or two heavier-weighted nymphs as droppers. These bounce on or close to the bottom.

SMALL FLY REEL
Small fly reels work best for Czech nymphing, as there is no need to hold lots of backing.

CZECH-NYMPHING TECHNIQUES

Study the river and work out where the fish will be. They may be feeding among rocks and boulders, or over gravel banks, so wade out close to where you want to fish. It is essential for you to enter the water so that you can flick the flies out the short distance required to maintain control of the short fly line as the flies drift downstream.

When Czech nymphing, fish with a short line to maintain direct contact with your flies. Strip a short length of line off your reel and make a simple sideways or overhead cast upstream to cover your chosen area on the drift down. Weighted flies sink quickly, so be alert the moment your line hits the water. The current will take your sinking flies downstream and through the places where you think the fish will be. The movement of the water will make the flies flutter and work, but you need to keep the rod high and allow the fly line to just touch the surface.

Bites vary, but be prepared to strike or lift into a fish at any time. While your flies may snag on rocks and give false bites, it is vital to concentrate hard and strike anything that looks like a bite.

1 **Pick the right flies** to imitate foods that species such as yellowfish, trout, or grayling may feed on underwater. Czech Nymph and Copper John flies work well. Look at the undersides of stones and small boulders to find out what is in the river, and what the fish are likely to be feeding on.

GRAVEL GUARDS

Some rivers are warm enough to permit wet wading (wading without chest waders). However, it is always advisable to wear felt-soled boots to protect your feet and give extra grip. It is also recommended that you wrap neoprene gravel guards around the bottoms of your calves and the tops of the boots to prevent stones and gravel from getting into your boots.

2 **Fish with a short line** to keep your flies close to the rod tip. Maintain contact as the flies drift downstream, then lift up and cast or flick again, covering as large an area of water as you can. Move around slowly and steadily.

3 **Be prepared to strike** or lift into a fish at any time. The strike indicator may suddenly disappear under the water, your line may visibly tighten, or the flies may stop suddenly. When you have landed a fish, unhook it, and release it carefully.

Sight-fishing for wild brown trout

Locating wild brown trout in crystal-clear rivers, and then casting small flies at them, is one of the purest forms of fly-fishing. Big wild brown trout are found in many parts of the world. They are often wary and tricky to catch, but the rewards of success are worth the effort.

ROD AND RIG SETUP

A 9-ft (2.7-m) fly rod rated #5 or #6, and a nonreflective fly reel, are perfect. Choose dull-colored, nonreflective, floating lines, matched to the rod rating. Clear, tapered leaders are essential, and may be up to 16 ft (5 m) long to avoid spooking the fish. Tailor rigs to local conditions. A good pair of polarized sunglasses is vital, and a wide-brimmed hat or a dull-colored baseball cap is also handy.

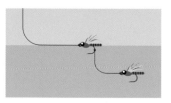

NEW ZEALAND DROPPER
Try using a New Zealand dropper rig. In this rig the dropper fly (often a nymph) is tied to the bend of the dry fly's hook. As well as fishing effectively, the dry fly acts as a strike-indicator for the wet fly.

HUMPY DRY FLY
The hair on the "hump" of this classic dry fly gives added buoyancy for fishing moving and often slightly turbulent water. The most commonly used sizes of Humpy flies are 10 to 18.

LOCATION AND PREPARATION

Sight-fishing calls for a stealthy approach because the fish will have a perfect line of sight to all approaching anglers. Wear dull-colored clothing and ensure that none of your fishing gear is reflective.

The largest numbers of fish will be in fairly shallow water, but it can take practice to spot them. Make sure you are wearing polarized sunglasses and concentrate hard on seeing "through" the water—often, in such clear water, there will be fish you simply do not see at first. A sound casting technique, involving as few false casts

as possible, will make it less likely that the fish will see your lines moving around; try to avoid using too many false casts.

In very clear water, wading is not advised because of the risk of spooking the fish, so position yourself as low down and as far back as you can, and step lightly on the river bank.

1 **Once you have spotted** trout, prepare to cover the area as efficiently as possible. Strip the required line from your reel, make a couple of false casts, and then quietly and smoothly drop the fly above the area, so that the current pulls it down over the fish. Mend the line (*see* p.94), if necessary, when it lands on the water—the aim is to have the fly drift naturally.

2 **Big, wild brown trout** can be extremely wary, and it often requires real skill even to put a fly over them, let alone successfully land one. If a fish does take your dry fly off the surface, make yourself hesitate for a second before striking—let the fish really take the fly properly. This is hard because seeing a fish come up is exciting. Wild trout are powerful and usually go on a run toward the nearest snag. Fight the fish hard, without breaking the leader, and maneuver yourself to put pressure on the fish.

3 **Bring the trout** over your waiting net, either alone, by tiring out the fish, or with the help of your guide. It is a challenge to do this with a rod in one hand and net in the other, but immensely satisfying when accomplished successfully.

Fly-fishing for Atlantic salmon

Anglers have fly-fished for Atlantic salmon for hundreds of years. Some large rivers are fished with double-handed fly rods and with graceful Spey casts (advanced roll casts with a large change of direction), whereas smaller rivers are better suited to smaller, single-handed rods.

ROD AND RIG SETUP

Choose a standard #8 single-handed fly rod and matched reel, or a #8 or #9 double-hander. You will need a rod that is light to handle, depending on where you fish. Floating lines are normally used, along with tapered leaders. Some rivers ban the use of weighted flies, so at times you will need to use a line with a weighted tip (sink-tip). You may be required to use barbless hooks.

SALMON-FISHING FLY REEL
A salmon reel that you intend to use for double-handed Spey casting has to be fairly large to hold the length and thickness of line needed. Reels for single-handed fly-fishing are smaller.

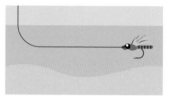

SINGLE-FLY RIG
Use a single weighted fly for salmon fishing. A heavily weighted tube fly is often used, to sink the fly as fast as possible, but often the sheer speed of the current means that the fly never sinks very deep.

LOCATION AND PREPARATION

Salmon stop feeding when they enter a river to head for their spawning grounds. Nobody knows whether they attack anglers' flies because of a feeding instinct, annoyance at the sight of a fly drifting past them again and again, competition among the school, or for some other reason. However, there is nothing complicated about fly-fishing for salmon; you just need to know where the fish will swim, and have the skill to cast and retrieve your fly.

It is worth securing the services of a good guide who knows the river well, for salmon are predictable in where they like to be. The fish will not stay in the fastest parts of the river, but will look for natural pools, or eddies.

Having chosen your spot, you need to put out your fly repeatedly, and let it fish with the river flow. Generally, flies are cast out across the stream, or slightly downstream, and allowed to swing naturally with the current, before being retrieved and cast again.

1 **Choose your fly carefully.** Many salmon anglers and guides have a favorite fly that tends to work well. Some use the same fly virtually all the time, and catch plenty of fish. Thinking anglers will change the fly after repeated casting, for the salmon will have seen, and possibly refused, the fly on many occasions. The theory is that a change of fly may produce a take.

2 **Cover the water by casting** your line either directly across the stretch of river, or slightly downstream. Then mend (adjust) the line, and allow the current to swing your fly across the water you want to fish. Let the fly hang for a while; when it has swung in close to the bank, strip back, and then cast again. The longer your fly spends in the water, the greater your chance of catching a salmon.

3 **Strike if the line suddenly tightens**. It is essential to keep a tight line in order to maintain the hook-hold when fighting the fish. Be sure to follow instructions from your guide on how to land the salmon.

4 **Take care of this magnificent fish** when unhooking it. Keep it in the water, turning the fish slightly on its side to help calm it down. A barbless hook is usually very easy to remove. Many salmon rivers operate a catch-and-release-only policy.

A FISH TO ADMIRE
Atlantic salmon are special fish, and the capture of a large specimen will be remembered for a long time. A darker coloration is an indication that the fish has been in the river for a while. When they first come in from the sea, they are a bright chrome-silver color, and often have sea lice on their bodies.

Fly-fishing for steelhead

Migratory rainbow trout are known the world over as steelhead. These magnificent fish are renowned fighters, and offer one of the greatest fly-fishing challenges. Fishing often takes place surrounded by some of the wildest and most majestic scenery imaginable.

ROD AND RIG SETUP

Long, double-handed rods and Spey-casting techniques are used on the big steelhead rivers. To cast heavy lines and flies, you need a long rod that will pick the line off the water and take it across the river. Try a 13- to 14-ft (3.9–4.2-m) #9 double-handed rod, with a large fly reel holding a floating Spey line and plenty of backing.

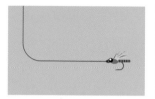

WET-FLY RIG
A tapered leader is looped to the end of the thick floating Spey line. The big fly will sink down into the water to a depth determined by the speed of the current.

STEELHEAD FLY
Most steelhead flies are large and brightly colored. This Purple String Leach is designed to appeal to the predatory instinct in the fish, and also to show up well in murky water. Big flies are hard to cast, so protect your eyes with sunglasses.

GOING STEELHEAD FISHING

Most of the famous steelhead rivers are in British Columbia, Canada, and along the west coast of the United States. There are various runs of fish during the year, but most traveling anglers choose to target steelhead in either spring or fall; locals also fish in the depths of winter. Fly-fishing for steelhead is similar to fly-fishing for salmon or big sea trout. You cast the fly out across the river, let the thick fly line swing the fly around in the current, then draw it in toward the bank. The big difference is that at least half the steelhead caught are taken "on the dangle"—this is when the fly swings in near the bank and the angler lets it hang there for a few seconds to allow the current to move the fly. Steelhead are looking for the least amount of current to battle as they head upriver, and this tends to be close to the river bank. Look for a consistent flow to the water with no great depth, and wade out to no more than calf or mid-thigh depth. Take warm, layered clothing with you to deal with the possibility of cold conditions, plus good-quality breathable chest waders and wading jacket.

1 Fish the dangle. Your natural reaction would be to cast again as the fly swings around in the current and in toward the river bank. Instead, allow the fly to hang in the current straight down your rod tip for at least ten seconds before casting out again.

2 **Play a fast-running steelhead hard**. Let the fish run when it wants to, but keep a bend in the rod at all times, and work on retrieving line when the fish tires and stops. Tuck a double-handed rod into your stomach for extra support.

3 **Land the steelhead** with a net. Be aware of keeping a tight line to the fish at all times, and work with your guide to bring the fish over the waiting net. A fly-angler will always release a steelhead; indeed, many rivers operate a barbless-hook-only, catch-and-release policy.

SAFE WADING

Wading is an essential part of fishing, so learn to wade safely. A wading belt pulls tight around your waders to slow the flow of water into the legs and feet if you fall. Wade slowly—watch how the river flows, then decide where to place your feet. Perceptions of depth can be misleading, so use a wading stick, or your rod, to measure the depth and help keep you stable as you wade out. Never wade beyond the point where you feel safe.

Fly-fishing for carp

Fishing for carp on fly-fishing tackle is perhaps not the purest form of fly-fishing, but it attracts modern anglers who are looking for a new challenge, and is fantastic fun. Carp often feed on or just below the surface, which makes them perfect for targeting on fly-fishing tackle.

ROD AND RIG SETUP

Use #7 to #9 fly rods and matched reels with a visible floating line and a fluorocarbon leader. Try to find out how big the carp you are fishing are likely to be, so you can plan your tackle needs. Use more powerful tackle if big carp are a possibility. Carp fly-fishing is often done in snaggy areas where it is important to be able to put pressure on running fish.

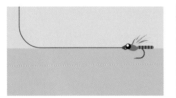

FLOATING-LINE RIG
You are mainly targeting carp that are feeding off the surface, so floating lines are essential. If the fly sinks after a while, add some floatant (normally a gel) to keep it on the surface.

BONIO CARP FLY
Use flies that resemble bread or dog biscuits. This small fly looks like a dog biscuit and will float on the surface among the real biscuits that have been introduced. The aim is to get the carp to eat it confidently.

LOCATION AND TIME

Don't target waters where there is huge pressure on only a few big carp. It is far better to fish where there are carp populations of all sizes that are willing to come up to the surface to feed. First and last light are the best times to find carp surface-feeding. Cloud cover and still conditions are also more likely to bring success than very bright sunlight on the water, which often drives fish to the bottom.

1 **Use the roll cast,** which does not entail a back-cast, to put out flies when casting room is restricted. Many small carp waters are surrounded by extensive vegetation, which makes for harder casting. The roll cast enables the fly-angler to put flies out a fair distance.

USING FLIES AND BAITS

Carp are extremely adept at feeding off the surface; their mouths are perfectly designed to suck in particles of food. With this in mind, it is worthwhile spending some time throwing bits of bread and dog biscuits into the water and watching their feeding habits. This technique is as useful to the fly-angler as it is to the bait- and lure-angler.

Fish that feed off the surface are often very wary, so approach stealthily— do not break natural horizons, wear relatively dull clothing (many carp anglers dress in camouflage colors), and keep noise to a minimum. Once the carp you aim to fish for are feeding happily and coming up for food on a regular basis, you can cast your fly in among the offerings, and wait for a bite.

STRIKING AND PLAYING

The secret is not to strike the moment you see a carp closing in on your bait, but rather to steel yourself to wait until it has very visibly engulfed your fly. Now strike and start playing the fish. Be very alert; carp are powerful fish that know their surroundings well—be prepared for a hard fight.

2 **Playing a carp** takes skill. When hooked, larger fish will be determined to reach snags, so it is vital to keep the rod bent into the fish. If the rod is hardly bent, the fish is not under enough pressure. Have a landing net and a carp bed close by.

3 **The safest and most humane way** to land carp is with a soft-meshed landing net on a long handle. Be sure to bring the carp over the landing net using the rod, rather than chasing the fish with the net. Many carp are lost by going after the fish and bumping the hook out or breaking the line.

Fly-fishing for pike

The pike is a hugely popular freshwater species, often caught with bait and lures, but increasing numbers of anglers from the fly-fishing world are realizing that this magnificent predator is also extremely eager to take flies. Pike offer a world-class fly-fishing challenge.

ROD AND RIG SETUP

Pike flies are heavy and the quarry can grow large, so use a #9 fly rod and reel. Saltwater fly rods of 9 ft (2.7 m) in length are perfect as they often have a fast action, which helps lines and flies to cut through the wind. Take reels or spools loaded with floating and intermediate lines for versatility. Make sure you carry an unhooking tool.

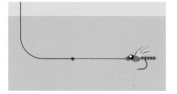

WIRE TRACE
Use a thin, flexible wire trace that is easy to tie, such as the coated variety. Flies are usually fished below the surface, but in warmer water pike will often take poppers and crease flies on the surface.

BUNNY BUG PIKE FLY
Big and bold, pike flies are not subtle. A Bunny Bug on a 2/0 or 3/0 hook is typical. Try different designs until you find one that works on the waters you are fishing.

CHOOSING YOUR LOCATION

Not all fly-fishing waters contain pike, and those that do may not allow anglers to fish for them. However, with their increased popularity, many fisheries are encouraging anglers to try their luck if pike are present. Large pike are solitary and like to lurk in cover and then pounce on their prey, so when you get to the lake, ask local anglers for tips and look for fish-holding features. If there are trout, which pike feed on, think about where they might be. The best places to start are near structures and cover— weed beds, sunken trees, or inlets—but don't forget, pike also feed in open water.

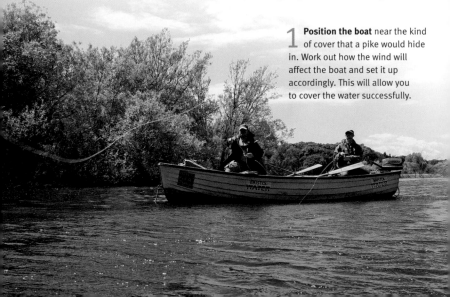

1 **Position the boat** near the kind of cover that a pike would hide in. Work out how the wind will affect the boat and set it up accordingly. This will allow you to cover the water successfully.

CASTING, STRIKING, AND PLAYING

It is essential to cover as much water as possible with your fly; the pike could be anywhere. Their keen senses will alert them to your fly in the water, so use powerful and efficient casting to keep it working for as long as possible. The basic overhead cast is sufficient, but more line speed will be built up to move a big fly through the air if you use a double-haul to the cast. Big flies are subject to wind resistance, so the faster you can move the fly in the cast, the farther it will go out and the more softly it will land on the water. You may see pike come at your fly and then suddenly turn away. If this happens, repeat the cast and retrieve a couple of times to see if the fish is interested—more often than not, it will be. When a pike takes the fly, it is almost like hitting a brick wall—everything suddenly stops and then a split-second later the fish usually charges off. There is often no time or need to strike, as a hungry pike will engulf the fly with ease. These fish are known for doing a lot of head-shaking during the fight, so keep a tight line to the fish at all times. Do not go out on the water without a buoyancy aid or lifejacket.

2 **Palming the reel** in conjuction with using the drag system on your reel is a simple way to apply more drag when fighting a fish. Use your hand to apply pressure to the spool, but take your hand away quickly if the fish suddenly starts to run. The technique is effective, but it takes some practice.

3 **Use a large soft-mesh net** for landing pike. These fish require delicate handling as they are often exhausted by the fight. Remove the hook with long-nose pliers at the side of the boat, or on board on a carp mat. Hold the pike in the water and wait for it to revive before letting it go.

Fly-fishing for bonefish

Many in-shore waters of the world's tropical regions consist of large areas of very shallow water where the bottom is generally hard sand, coral, mud, and turtle grass. These "flats" are home to bonefish, a species that is hugely adept at feeding in such "skinny" water.

ROD AND RIG SETUP

Fishing very shallow water calls for floating fly lines, plenty of backing to deal with fast-running fish, and a long, tapered leader. A #8 or #9 fly-fishing rod and matching reel will serve you perfectly on the flats, but above all, make sure the drag system on your reel can cope with the explosive run of a hooked bonefish. Few fish run as fast when hooked, making this fish one of the ultimate saltwater prizes for fly-anglers.

SINGLE-FLY RIG
Bonefish are fished for with single, weighted flies that are gently retrieved along the bottom, where the bonefish feed when they are on the flats.

CLOUSER MINNOW
Available in several colors, of which this is one of the most common, the Clouser Minnow is highly effective for catching bonefish. The weighted eyes invert the fly as it is twitched along the bottom. Carry various colors in your fly box.

TARGETING BONEFISH

Without doubt some of the most exciting and visual fishing there is, fly-fishing on saltwater flats is all about being able to see the fish that you are casting at. Fishing in very shallow water calls for an array of different skills that will put any angler to the test. An essential part of your kit is a pair of good polarized sunglasses, which will help you to see through the water by cutting the glare.

Bonefish, a common species in shallow tropical waters, are easily spooked, which calls for a very measured approach. Stalk them slowly and quietly, watching out for moving schools of fish and movement on the surface of the water. Bonefish feed hard on the bottom and when they put their heads down to do this, their tails often become visible as they break the surface of the water. Known as "tailing," this is an unmistakable sign of the presence of bonefish.

Step gently and slowly to enable you to get within casting range of the fish. Generally, you will aim to cast in front of the fish, but be careful not to alarm them by allowing your line to land over them. Bonefish are celebrated for being a very "honest" fish. This refers to the fact that if you make the right cast in the right place, more often than not the fish will take your fly.

1 **Fish with an experienced guide,** to help you spot the bonefish. The more you fish the flats, the better you will become at seeing fish, but a good guide will always spot more fish than you, and will advise on exactly where to cast and how to fish the fly.

2 **Cast fast, accurate lines** to avoid spooking the fish. A tight loop shows a good fly-casting style. In these locations, there is often a breeze, so the more proficient you are at casting, the more likely you are to succeed in placing flies where the bonefish can see them.

3 **When a bonefish takes the fly**, set the hook as fast as you can. Lift the rod high in order to keep the line away from the coral. Bonefish will run very fast when hooked, and may do so repeatedly.

4 **To land the fish**, most fly-anglers bring their catch to hand when it begins to tire. Even so, it may still charge off again, so be ready to grab the fish, calm it down, remove the hook, then gently release it unharmed.

Fly-fishing from a flats boat

Many of the world's saltwater flats systems are successfully fly-fished from skiffs or flats boats, and catches can be spectacular. Shallow-draft, fast boats make it possible to fish a lot of water, and to move to a different spot quickly if the fish are not biting.

ROD AND RIG SETUP

Permit, snook, and bonefish can be fished for with #8 fly-fishing rods, or #9 for larger permit. Tarpon demand a #12 rod if big fish are expected; they are uncontrollable on anything less, for all but the most experienced anglers. Floating lines are required to fish the flats, and use a single fly for permit, snook, and tarpon fishing.

CHARTREUSE-AND-WHITE CLOUSER MINNOW
One of the world's most consistently successful flies for saltwater fly-fishing, the Clouser Minnow imitates various baitfish. The chartreuse-and-white version works well for tarpon and snook. Clouser Minnows can also work for permit, but generally these fish prefer crab patterns.

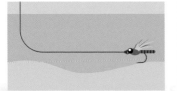

FLATS-FISHING SETUP
Use a single fly. For permit, try a weighted crab pattern and cast just in front of the fish, then twitch back toward you. Tarpon will take large flies just under the surface.

PERMIT FISHING

Permit are among the most sought-after flats species, and to take a permit on the fly is a serious challenge. They can be choosy when presented with a fly and simply refuse all fly patterns; or they may spook immediately. However, when one finally goes tail up and takes a fly, the lucky angler is about to engage in one of the most spectacular fights it is possible to have on a fly rod.

ON THE FLATS

Many of the world's best flats-fishing destinations offer fishing from skiffs, with competent and knowledgeable guides who will go out of their way to help you. While the aim is to take you to the fishing grounds fast, the special advantage of a flats boat is the poling platform at the back of the boat—once you are on the flats and near the fish, the guide will cut the engine, raise it, and take position on the platform. Guides on these boats generally use a long, generally carbon-fiber pole to move you around quietly. Standing high up, and therefore able to spot fish more easily, they brief you with a series of simple instructions. Keep your spare line coiled neatly on the casting platform, and be ready to cast an accurate line at all times (remembering your guide is standing behind you). It is often possible to creep up close to fish, and the closer you can get, the easier the cast, especially when there is a wind blowing. In time, you will learn to see the fish really well and cast accordingly.

1 **Stow your gear safely** for the journey to the flats, as the boats go extremely fast over shallow water. Often your guide will take the boat through a maze of mangroves and channels—on extensive flats systems, the fish can be spread out in different areas.

2 **Cast as close as you can** to the spot your guide advises. The faster you can place a fly in front of the fish, the better your chance of connecting; the fish are constantly moving and you may get only one chance. Double-hauling (*see* pp.62–63) is a useful skill in this situation.

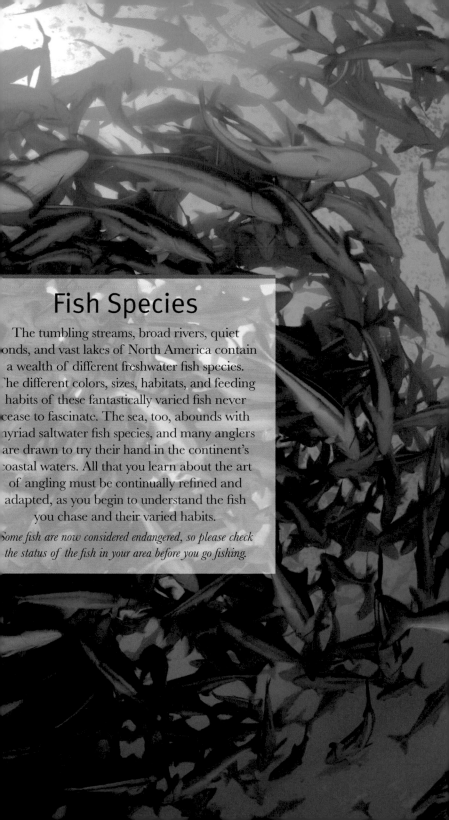

Fish Species

The tumbling streams, broad rivers, quiet
ponds, and vast lakes of North America contain
a wealth of different freshwater fish species.
The different colors, sizes, habitats, and feeding
habits of these fantastically varied fish never
cease to fascinate. The sea, too, abounds with
myriad saltwater fish species, and many anglers
are drawn to try their hand in the continent's
coastal waters. All that you learn about the art
of angling must be continually refined and
adapted, as you begin to understand the fish
you chase and their varied habits.

*Some fish are now considered endangered, so please check
the status of the fish in your area before you go fishing.*

Salmo trutta (freshwater)

Brown trout
and Sea trout

WEIGHT Up to 110 lb (50 kg).

TYPES OF WATER Streams, rivers, lakes, and reservoirs; coastal waters (sea trout).

DISTRIBUTION Temperate regions worldwide.

FISHING METHOD Primarily fly-fishing, but can also be caught with bait and lures.

The brown trout (*Salmo trutta*, morpha: *fario*), and its seagoing form the sea trout (*Salmo trutta*, morpha: *trutta*) is one of the most important game-fishing species and is found throughout the world. The species is native to Europe and western Asia, but over hundreds of years it has been gradually introduced into many other temperate regions. The brown trout has a brownish body with distinct red and black spots, but there are many variations according to habitat and genetic makeup. This species can be found in a variety of waters, from the smallest streams to large lakes and reservoirs. It feeds principally on insects, larvae, and small fish. At times, as most trout anglers discover, this species can be extremely choosy about what it will eat.

SEA TROUT

The sea trout is a silvery-blue-colored, migratory form of brown trout that spends its early life in freshwater, but enters the sea between the ages of one and five years. It eventually returns to the rivers to spawn. The preference of this form of the species is for cold, fast-flowing water. During its river-dwelling phase, the sea trout gradually darkens, but never reverts completely to the coloration of a brown trout. Unlike the Atlantic salmon, the sea trout does not

FLY-FISHING FOR BROWN TROUT
Crystal-clear rivers and streams provide an ideal environment for brown trout. Fly-fishing in such waters requires patience and skill.

need floodwater to move up the spawning rivers. However, a river in spate does tend to attract this species in large numbers. The sea trout often moves most confidently at night, and the best fishing for this species tends to be at the end of the day. Some anglers prefer to fish for sea trout after dark.

Black and red spots

Brown trout

Silver-blue coloration

Spots above and below lateral line

Squared-off tail

Sea trout

CANNIBAL BROWN TROUT

Large, predatory brown trout are known as ferox, or cannibal, trout. Once thought to be a different species, it is now known that these are simply brown trout that have changed to a diet based mainly on fish—sometimes including small members of their own species. The ferox trout has a hooked jaw and lives longer than most brown trout.

Ferox trout

Oncorhynchus mykiss (freshwater)

Rainbow trout
and Steelhead

WEIGHT Up to 55 lb (25 kg).

TYPES OF WATER Rivers, lakes; coastal waters (steelhead).

DISTRIBUTION Temperate waters worldwide.

FISHING METHOD Fly-fishing, less commonly bait- and lure-fishing.

The rainbow trout and its seagoing form (both *Oncorhynchus mykiss*) are among the principal game-fishing quarries, and have been introduced in temperate waters worldwide. The species includes many subspecies, including the Kamloops, Kern River, and Shasta rainbow trout. Great numbers are successfully bred in lakes and reservoirs, but there are various wild strains that spend their lives in rivers and, if allowed, will run to the sea and ultimately return to the rivers to spawn. Rainbow trout that have migrated to sea are known as steelhead. Any stock of rainbow trout can migrate like this if given the chance.

PHYSICAL CHARACTERISTICS

Rainbow trout vary hugely in appearance but they are distinguished by a pink stripe along the lateral line. They are speckled black along their sides, back, upper fins, and tail. In North America, rainbow trout can reach up to 55 lb (25 kg), but in Europe, they more commonly reach a maximum weight of around 24 lb (11 kg). They feed mainly on insects and their larvae and may also take crustaceans, fish eggs, and small fish. Wild rainbow trout are known for being hard fighters when hooked.

STEELHEAD FISHING

Steelhead are famous among fly-anglers for their intense silvery coloration and their impressive and powerful fighting abilities. The longer a sea-run steelhead

CUTTHROAT TROUT

This relative of the rainbow trout is native to western North America. It can be identified primarily by the telltale red "cutthroat" mark that is found under the chin and the pronounced black spots over much of the body. The overall body color of this species varies from mainly dark green to green-blue on the back.

Cutthroat trout

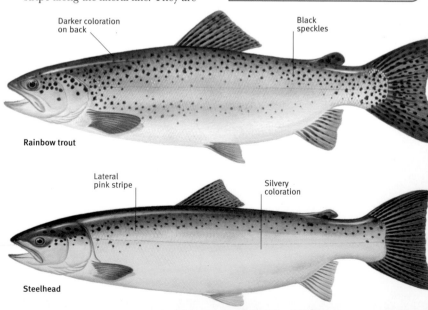

Darker coloration on back

Black speckles

Rainbow trout

Lateral pink stripe

Silvery coloration

Steelhead

spends in the river, the more its appearance tends to revert to that of a "standard" rainbow trout.

Without doubt, the most famous steelhead fishing in the world occurs in British Columbia on the west coast of Canada, where the fall runs of bright chrome fish are legendary. Steelhead smolts (two- or three-year-old fish) inhabit the Pacific waters along the west coast of North America, feeding on schools of small fish from Alaska down to Mexico. The larger fish are the most successful at returning to the rivers to spawn. Fly-fishing is the most popular way to target steelhead, mainly when they are returning from the sea to spawn.

STEELHEAD AND RIVER HEALTH

Observation of steelhead populations is a useful way to measure the health of a river system. In order to thrive, steelhead need cold, clear water, so fluctuations in their numbers often point toward problems with the waters of a river, such as increased pollution. This is important not only from a wildlife conservation perspective, but also for the prosperity of an area. An abundance of steelhead brings more anglers to an area, and more money into the local economy.

STEELHEAD RIVER
The rivers of northern California are known for their steelhead. For the fly-angler, these stunning locations can provide an unrivaled experience.

Salvelinus namaycush (freshwater)

Lake trout

WEIGHT Up to 70 lb (33 kg).

TYPES OF WATER Lakes, streams.

DISTRIBUTION North America; introduced to South America, Asia, and Europe.

FISHING METHODS Lure- and fly-fishing.

Lake trout can reach up to 5 ft (1.5 m) in length, with a distinctly forked tail, and do not have the dark spots of most other trout species. They are usually found in lakes and streams, and are fast-swimming, aggressive predators, feeding on all kinds of organisms from plankton to small mammals. Adult lake trout are known to eat smaller lake trout. They spawn when they reach the age of five to six years. The females release their eggs over the rocky bottoms of lakes. This enables the eggs to lie in crevices on the bottom. Fly-fishing and spinning are the favorite fishing methods, but many anglers prefer to troll lures behind boats.

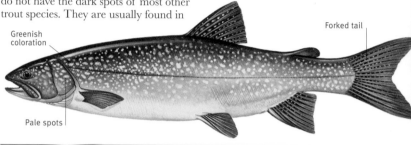

Greenish coloration

Forked tail

Pale spots

Salvelinus malma (freshwater)

Dolly varden

WEIGHT Up to 40 lb (18.5 kg).

TYPES OF WATER Lakes, and rivers; migrating to sea.

DISTRIBUTION North America; Arctic Ocean; northeastern and northwestern Pacific Ocean.

FISHING METHODS Lure-, bait-, and fly-fishing.

Dolly varden are part of the char family. They grow to about 4¼ ft (1.3 m) in length, and their light spots distinguish them from trout and salmon. Mature male dolly varden develop a distinctive bright red coloration along the lower body, and their fins take on a red-black tinge with white edges; over time they develop an extended lower jaw. Mature females are similar in color but less bright. Sea-going dolly varden are more silvery, with plenty of red-orange spots

MIGRATORY BEHAVIOR IN ALASKA

Dolly varden from northern Alaska tend to overwinter in rivers, whereas south-Alaskan dolly varden spend the winter in lakes. It is believed that they search for lakes on a random basis, by swimming up various rivers until they find one with a lake at the top. Both male and female dolly varden must return for spawning to the river in which they were spawned themselves.

on their flanks, and a greenish brown dorsal fin. Dolly varden spawn in streams during fall; the eggs are deposited in channels dug out by the females with their tails. The young migrate to sea at three or four years old, during May and June. Migrating fish then overwinter in freshwater, with distinct river and lake populations.

Light spots

Dark, reddish fins

Salvelinus alpinus (freshwater)

Arctic char

WEIGHT Up to 35 lb (15 kg).

TYPES OF WATER Clean, cold lakes and large rivers; some migrating to sea.

DISTRIBUTION North America; Arctic Ocean; Scandinavia; Iceland; Greenland; northern North Atlantic Ocean; occasionally northern UK.

FISHING METHODS Lure-, bait-, and fly-fishing.

All species of char have light spots on a dark overall coloration. Although similar to dolly varden, Arctic char have shorter heads and snouts, and their tails have a deeper fork. These fish can reach a maximum length of about 3¼ ft (1 m). Their backs are dark brown or olive,

CLEAN-WATER SPECIES
Arctic char need uncontaminated, well-oxygenated water to survive. This means that the best fishing is in the unspoiled waters of the north.

with lighter sides fading to a light-colored belly. Colors vary considerably at spawning time, especially in male Arctic char—the whole body may become gold or orange in color, and the lower fins often develop white edges. This species is believed to spawn in alternate years from August to October.

Arctic char are a popular angling quarry in the lakes of Kodiak Island in Alaska. They also congregate in the big lakes throughout Bristol Bay in Alaska from May to July, to feed on the salmon smolts that migrate toward the sea at this time.

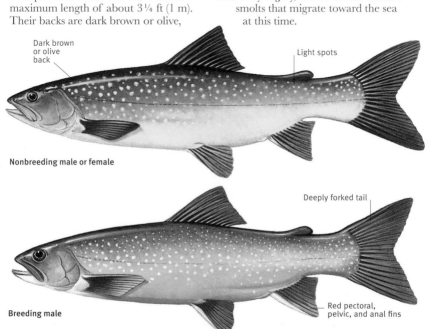

Dark brown or olive back

Light spots

Nonbreeding male or female

Deeply forked tail

Breeding male

Red pectoral, pelvic, and anal fins

Salmo salar (freshwater)

Atlantic salmon

WEIGHT Up to 105 lb (47 kg).

TYPES OF WATER Cold, fast-flowing rivers.

DISTRIBUTION North Atlantic, Baltic, and Arctic Ocean; introduced to Australasia and Argentina.

FISHING METHODS Fly-fishing.

The Atlantic salmon is a hugely important game fish and a highly prized catch, especially among fly-anglers. These fish can grow to large sizes and are extremely powerful swimmers, built for endurance and speed.

Before Atlantic salmon spawn, they spend several years feeding in the cold ocean waters, but once the urge to spawn comes, they return to the rivers in which they were born. A proportion of adult Atlantic salmon die after spawning, but some survive and these return to the sea. Young salmon (smolts) migrate to the sea after about two years.

Atlantic salmon stocks worldwide are under increasing commercial pressure, and the salmon-farming industry is expanding to satisfy the immense demand for this fish. However, there are places where sport-fishing for Atlantic salmon can still be truly excellent, such as the Kola Peninsula in northern Russia, parts of eastern Canada, and some of the great Norwegian salmon-river systems.

Various fishing methods are used, but fly-fishing is the most popular. Atlantic salmon do not feed during the return journey to their spawning rivers, so the angler must tempt them to take the fly.

Spotted above lateral line

Pale underside

LEAPING SALMON
Atlantic salmon returning to their native rivers to spawn must swim against the flow of the river. They often leap spectacularly up rocky falls or other obstructions to reach the spawning grounds.

Micropterus salmoides (freshwater)

Largemouth bass

WEIGHT Up to 22 lb (10 kg).

TYPES OF WATER Lakes, ponds, rivers, and creeks.

DISTRIBUTION North America from Canada to northern Mexico.

FISHING METHODS Bait-, lure-, and fly-fishing.

A member of the black bass family, which are active and sometimes cannibalistic predators, the largemouth bass has an upper jaw that extends to behind its eye, hence the name. This species feeds predominantly on smaller fish, frogs, and crayfish, but does not feed during spawning. As the water warms up, so does its metabolism: the preferred temperatures for feeding are from 50 to 80°F (10–27°C); it feeds most heavily from 68 to 80°F (20–27°C). Like all species of black bass, the largemouth bass thrives in clear water with either

LARGEMOUTH BASS
Largemouth bass prefer tranquil, clear waters where they can search for prey among the small fish and other creatures that hide in reeds or among bankside vegetation.

overgrown banks or extensive reed beds. The biggest largemouth bass are found in the rivers of Florida. A whole industry has grown up in the United States around these immensely popular fish, with professional tournament circuits and huge prize money to be won.

OTHER BLACK BASS SPECIES

The smallmouth bass (*Micropterus dolomieui*), distinguished by a jaw that does not extend farther than the eye, is a renowned hard-fighting fish. The spotted bass (*Micropterus punctulatus*) is named after the dark spots along the flank and belly areas, and a dark spot on the gill cover. Its mouth does not extend beyond the eye. It is found mainly in the Mississippi and Ohio river basins.

Spiny first dorsal fin ⎯⎯⎯⎯⎯⎯⎯⎯⎯⎯⎯⎯⎯⎯⎯ Soft-rayed second dorsal fin

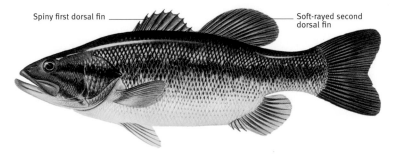

Ameiurus melas (freshwater)

Black bullhead

WEIGHT Up to 8 lb (3.6 kg).

TYPES OF WATER Rivers, streams, ponds, and lakes.

DISTRIBUTION Montana east to the Great Lakes and south to the Gulf Slope drainages.

FISHING METHODS Bait-, lure-, and fly-fishing.

The North American bullhead and freshwater catfish (*right*) are members of the Ictaluridae, which, with some 40 species, is the largest family of freshwater fish native to North America. Bullhead are omnivorous, bottom-feeding fish, found mostly in still and slow-flowing waters. They spawn in spring and early summer, laying their eggs in depressions in the mud or among stones and other cover. One or both parents will then guard the eggs until they hatch.

Bullhead are characterized by a large, bulbous head, a scaleless body, four pairs of barbels (whiskery extensions growing from the mouth), and an adipose fin. In addition, there are stiff, sharp spines at the leading edges of the pectoral and dorsal fins.

The black bullhead, also known as the horned pout, is the potentially largest of the bullhead species. While it can reach 8 lb (3.6 kg) in weight, it usually does not exceed 2 lb (910 g). This popular angling fish is often found over over soft, silty mud, and will tolerate very poor water quality. It is broadly similar in appearance to the brown bullhead (*Ameiurus nebulosus*), but it lacks the mottled coloration and large pectoral spine teeth of that species. The brown's maximum weight is only 5½ lb (2.5 kg), its average weight of about 3 lb (3.6 kg) is slightly more than that of the black. Other members of this group include the yellow bullhead (*Ameiurus natalis*), the flat bullhead (*Ameiurus platycephalus*), the spotted bullhead (*Ameiurus serracanthus*), and the snail bullhead (*Ameiurus brunneus*).

Bullhead can be caught with most natural or processed baits by float fishing, and also on small artificial lures by spinning or baitcasting. Try lightweight spinners and spoons, plastic worms, tiny jigs, and small wet flies. Adding small amounts of flavorings, such as spice oils, helps to make bread and other bland baits more attractive to the fish.

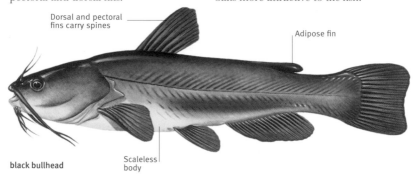

Dorsal and pectoral fins carry spines

Adipose fin

Scaleless body

black bullhead

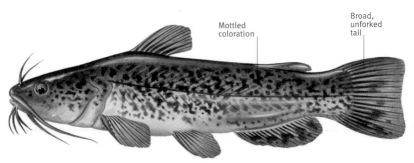

Mottled coloration

Broad, unforked tail

brown bullhead

Ictalurus furcatus (freshwater)

Blue catfish

WEIGHT Up to 100 lb (45 kg).
TYPES OF WATER Rivers, occasionally lakes.
DISTRIBUTION Mississippi basin, Gulf Slope drainages.
FISHING METHODS Bait-, lure-, and fly-fishing.

Like bullheads, catfish have scaleless bodies, broad heads, and whiskerlike barbels around their mouths. Catfish typically inhabit still or slow-flowing waters, and are most active at night and on cloudy days.

The blue catfish is the largest North American catfish, averaging up to 50 lb (22.7 kg) and capable of reaching 100 lb (45 kg). Unlike most other catfish, this species prefers swift-flowing, relatively clear streams to slow, turbid waters, and is found over rock, sand, or gravel bottoms rather than mud or silt. At night, blue catfish move from deep water into shallow, swift-flowing rapids and chutes to hunt for fish and crayfish. Other notable North american catfish include the flathead

SENSORY BARBELS

The barbels or "whskers" around the mouth of a catfish or bullhead are highly sensitive organs with which the fish can taste, smell, and feel its food—essential tools for a bottom-feeding fish. American catfish and bullhead have eight barbels; the Eurpoean wels catfish of the Siluridae family, shown above, has six.

catfish (*Pylodictis olivaris*) and the Channel catfish (*Ictalurus puncatatus*).

Freshwater catfish can be taken on practically any type of bait or lure, even a bare, shiny hook. In terms of bait, the best results are said to come with "stink" baits, such as soured clams, ripened chicken entrails, or coagulated blood.

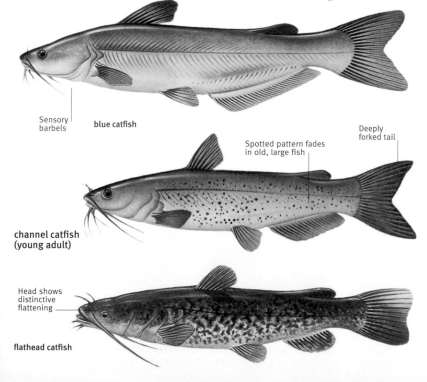

Sensory barbels | **blue catfish**

Deeply forked tail

Spotted pattern fades in old, large fish

channel catfish (young adult)

Head shows distinctive flattening

flathead catfish

Common carp

WEIGHT Up to 80 lb (37 kg).

TYPES OF WATER Large bodies of slow-moving or still water, such as natural and artificial lakes; prefers an environment with a soft or muddy bottom.

DISTRIBUTION Europe and Asia; introduced in North America, Australia, and New Zealand.

FISHING METHODS Bait-fishing (float-fishing, freelining, or bottom-fishing); also fly-fishing with imitation flies.

CAUGHT AND RELEASED
Large carp in protected waters are usually returned carefully to the water after being caught, to give other anglers the chance of good sport. They may live to be caught and released many times.

The common (or king) carp is an immensely popular fishing quarry throughout Europe, and is growing more popular in other

Scaleless head

Deep body

Barbels

CARP IN THE SHALLOWS
Extremely adept at swimming and feeding close to cover, carp are often found among the vegetation near to the bank.

areas of the world, including North America. Part of the attraction of this species as a target for anglers is the fact that individuals can grow to a very large size. In warm, food-rich waters, carp grow fast and can easily put on about 2 lb (1 kg) in weight every year.

The common carp is a deep-bodied fish. It has no scales on the head, but its body is covered with them. The varied diet of this species includes plants, insects, worms, and crustaceans, which it sucks in with a vacuumlike action. The common carp can spawn only when the water temperature rises to about 64°F (18°C). These long-lived fish can reach an age of more than 40 years old.

The common carp has evolved after hundreds of years of selective breeding. There are three varieties of common carp that are fished for, the standard common carp, the mirror carp (*see* panel, right), and the leather carp. The crucian carp (*Carassius carassius*), a separate species, is a popular target among some freshwater anglers. Highly tolerant of variable conditions, it lives in ponds and lakes and burrows into the mud during dry periods or in winter.

CARP VARIETIES

The common carp is descended from the wild carp that were introduced from Asia to Europe for food purposes during the Middle Ages. Found in only a few waters today, wild carp have a more elongated body and usually weigh under 15 lb (7 kg). The mirror carp, a variety of the modern common carp, is completely covered with large, irregularly shaped scales. There are a number of types of mirror carp; the linear type (*below*) has a distinct line of scales along its lateral line.

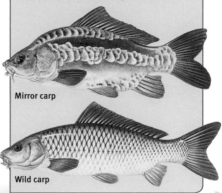

Mirror carp

Wild carp

Esox niger (freshwater)

Chain pickerel

WEIGHT Up to 9⅜ lb (4.25 kg).

TYPES OF WATER Clear rivers, streams, and stillwaters with abundant plant cover.

DISTRIBUTION Atlantic drainages from Nova Scotia to Florida, Mississippi basin from Missouri south.

FISHING METHODS Bait-, lure-, and fly-fishing.

Belonging to the pike family, the chain pickerel averages only 2 lb (910 g) but has been known to reach nearly 9½ lb (4.3 kg). Despite being relatively small, it provides good sport on light tackle, as do the even smaller grass pickerel (*Esox americanus vermiculatus*) and redfin pickerel (*Esox americanus americanus*), which are less than half its size. Besides the size difference, the chain pickerel can be distinguished from the grass and redfin by its markings. The chain pickerel has a distinctive dark, chainlike pattern on its sides, while the grass and redfin are both marked with dark bars; the redfin, as its name implies, also has red fins.

Like muskellunge (*below*) and northern pike (*right*), chain pickerels are admired by anglers because of the tenacious fight they put up when hooked. Small spinners and spoons (*see* p.39) are ideal for these fish. Fishing for chain pickerels through the ice is popular in the northeastern United States.

Chainlike patterns on sides

Esox masquinongy (freshwater)

Muskellunge

WEIGHT Up to 100 lb (45 kg).

TYPES OF WATER Lakes, ponds, and slow rivers and streams with thick vegetation.

DISTRIBUTION Great Lakes region, Mississippi basin, Atlantic drainages south to Georgia and Virginia.

FISHING METHODS Bait-, lure-, and fly-fishing.

The mighty muskellunge is a powerful, fast-growing fish that can reach a length of 12 in (30 cm) in only four months and grows to 6 ft (1.8 m) or more. It is a member of the pike family and, like all pike, it is a voracious predator. The principal food of the pike family is fish, but given the chance they will also take other aquatic prey, including frogs, snakes, crayfish, rodents, and ducklings.

The "muskie" is a popular quarry for anglers that can grow larger than its close relative, the northern pike (*right*). The most visible difference between the two species is in their markings: the muskie has dark bars or blotches on its sides, while the pike carries a series of pale bars and spots.

Muskellunge are active predators, and they are usually caught by spinning, baitcasting, and trolling, using lures, deadbaits, and livebaits. Fish for them from the bank or use a boat to reach weedbeds that are otherwise inaccessible.

Dark bars and blotches differentiate muskellunge from northern pike

Abundant sharp teeth

Esox lucius (freshwater)

Northern pike

WEIGHT Up to 75 lb (35 kg).

TYPES OF WATER Quiet lakes, ponds, and rivers; occasionally brackish waters.

DISTRIBUTION North America, Europe, central Asia.

FISHING METHODS Bait-, lure-, and fly-fishing.

The northern pike is an extremely adept, streamlined predator. Its body is designed principally for intense bursts of high speed, while a long, flat snout, plenty of extremely sharp teeth, and complex jaws enable it to take relatively large prey up to 25 percent of its own body weight. This fish prefers a solitary existence, and it is a skillful and aggressive feeder, often using weeds for cover. It can also be cannibalistic, attacking smaller fish of its own species. The pike inhabits clear lakes, ponds, and rivers, and is

A CAMOUFLAGED HUNTER
The barred and spotted markings of the northern pike give good camouflage for this voracious predator, hiding among weed beds. Its sharp teeth are able to deal with quite large prey.

considered a territorial fish. On some coastlines, the northern pike enters brackish water to feed on sea fish.

This is one of the few freshwater species to be native to both North America and Eurasia. It is generally accepted that some of the largest pike are to be found in the larger lochs of Scotland and Ireland. Most of the specimens caught are much smaller than the maximum recorded weight: 10 to 20 lb (4.5–9 kg) is more common for line-caught pike. Northern pike are usually targeted with baits and lures. Some massive pike have also been caught on fly-fishing tackle. Their sharp teeth require the use of wire traces.

Protruding
lower jaw

Perca flavescens (freshwater)

Yellow perch

WEIGHT Up to 4¼ lb (1.9 kg).

TYPES OF WATER Streams, lakes, and ponds,

DISTRIBUTION From Northwest Territories to the Atlantic drainages as far south as South Carolina.

FISHING METHODS Bait-fishing (float-fishing and bottom-fishing), lure-fishing (spinning).

The Percidae is a large, diverse family of fish comprising perch and related species such as walleye and sauger.

The North American yellow perch both looks and behaves very much like the European perch, and the two are closely related. It is a schooling fish that feeds on small fish and aquatic invertebrates, and is itself an important food source for predators such as walleye, northern pike, and muskellunge (*see* pp.126–27).

Like all the larger members of the Percidae, yellow perch make excellent eating and are among the tastiest of freshwater fish. Worms and maggots are good bait for perch. When spinning, use spinners, spoons, jigs, and plugs.

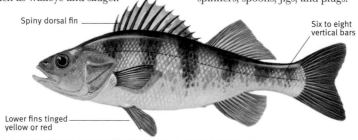

Spiny dorsal fin

Six to eight vertical bars

Lower fins tinged yellow or red

Stizostedion vitreum (freshwater)

Walleye

WEIGHT Up to 25 lb (11.3 kg).

TYPES OF WATER Deep waters in large streams and lakes.

DISTRIBUTION Northwest Territories east to Quebec, southeast to Alabama.

FISHING METHODS Bait-fishing (float-fishing and bottom-fishing) and lure-fishing (spinning).

The walleye is so named because of its large, glassy eyes, which are distinctive in daylight and glow at night when a light is shone upon them, like the eyes of a cat.

The walleye is the largest of the North American perches, typically reaching 3 lb (1.4 kg) but with a maximum of 25 lb (11.3 kg). Like other perch, it has a long,

PIKEPERCH

The walleye, the North American sauger (*Stizostedion canadense*), and the European zander (*Stizostedion lucioperca*) are together known as pikeperch. There are only slight genetic differences between these species, and they all similar in appearance and habit.

Sauger

slender body and feels rough to the touch, because its scales have teeth on their exposed edges. This is a prized food fish, as well as a favorite quarry of anglers. Angling techniques are similar to those used for yellow perch (*above*).
Use small fish for bait.

Dorsal fins separate, not joined as in some Percidae

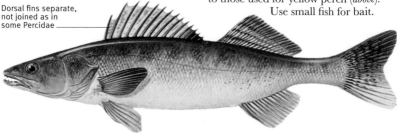

Morone mississippiensis (freshwater)

Yellow bass

WEIGHT Up to 2½ lb (1.1 kg).

TYPES OF WATER Quiet pools of rivers and lakes.

DISTRIBUTION From Montana and Wisconsin south to the Gulf of Mexico.

FISHING METHODS Lure-fishing (spinning) and fly-fishing.

This little freshwater bass lives in schools, feeding on fish, crustaceans, and insects from the mid-depths to the surface. It has silvery yellow sides, and the lower stripes along the its flanks are broken and offset.

The yellow bass rarely exceeds 2½ lb (1.1 kg), and usually weighs only 4 to 12 oz (113 to 240 g). Despite its small size, it offers good sport on light tackle. These fish are active predators, and will take most suitably sized natural or artificial baits.

The white bass (*Morone chrysops*) is similar to the yellow, but its coloration is silvery white, its stripes are not broken, and its lower jaw is more protuberant. It can grow to over 6½ lb (3 kg), but most of those caught are 2 lb (910 g) or less.

Until recently, these perchlike species and others in the *Morone* genus were considered part of the Percichthyidae family, but now they are classified as a separate family, the Moronidae.

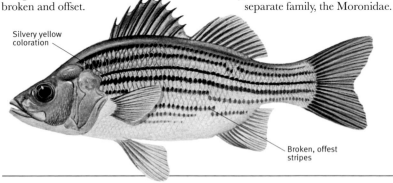

Silvery yellow coloration

Broken, offest stripes

Tinca tinca (freshwater)

Tench

WEIGHT Up to 16 lb (7.5 kg).

TYPES OF WATER Slow-moving or still water in ponds, lakes, or rivers.

DISTRIBUTION Europe and Asia, introduced into North America and Australia.

FISHING METHODS Predominantly bait-fishing, usually float-fishing or bottom-fishing.

Introduced into North America, tench are especially popular in their native Europe. The are famed for being dogged fighters when hooked. Tench live in relatively

warm ponds and lakes, but they can also inhabit the slow-moving or still lower sections of some rivers. They feed hardest around dawn, on the edge of dense vegetation such as reed beds. During winter, tench are known to remain in the mud and not feed.

Tench breed in shallow water, and the larvae remain attached to plants for a few days after hatching. They are slow-growing fish and their small scales are covered in a dense layer of protective slime. Male tench have a longer pelvic fin than females. Dawn is traditionally considered by anglers to be the best time of day for tench fishing.

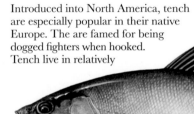

Small barbel

Tiny scales

Thymallus thymallus (freshwater)

Grayling

WEIGHT Up to 15 lb (6.7 kg).

TYPES OF WATER Rivers, occasionally lakes.

DISTRIBUTION Northern North America and northern Europe.

FISHING METHODS Bait-, lure-, and fly-fishing.

The grayling is not a particularly large fish, growing to a maximum of about 2 ft (60 cm) in length, but it has a highly distinctive, large dorsal fin. It is very gregarious, forming schools, and prefers to live in well-oxygenated, running water. It is commonly found in rivers, and in North America it can be found in lakes. It is particularly susceptible to pollution and thrives best in clean water, usually in the upper parts of a river with a gravel or sandy bottom. It feeds predominantly on a varied diet of insects, nymphs, worms, and crustaceans.

The grayling spawns in spring and early summer and does so in gravel-bottomed, shallow parts of the river. Grayling of the North American lakes come into

DWARFING

In waters where large numbers of grayling congregate, the amount of food available to each fish is limited, and small, deep-bodied individuals, with a weight no more than half the maximum recorded, are common. The large dorsal fin still gives the fish extra leverage against the angler, making the grayling a popular catch.

the streams for spawning. The use of small lures or spinners, or baits, are among the most common methods used to target fish of this species. Fly-fishing techniques can also be effective.

Large dorsal fin

DISTINCTIVE DORSAL FIN
The oversized dorsal fin becomes more highly colored in the breeding season and is used by the male grayling to wrap over the female during spawning.

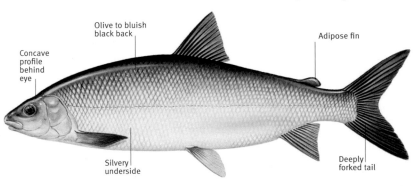

Coregonus clupeaformis (freshwater)

Lake whitefish

WEIGHT Up to 20 lb (9 kg).

TYPES OF WATER Lakes and streams.

DISTRIBUTION Throughout Alaska, Canada, and the northern United States.

FISHING METHODS Bait-, lure-, and fly-fishing.

Like grayling, whitefish are widely distributed in the colder lakes and streams of the Northern Hemisphere. Although some whitefish are popular angling species, numerous whitefish are threatened with extinction, and it is illegal to fish for them in many countries and on certain waters.

While it is primarily a lake-dwelling species, the lake whitefish also enters rivers. It feeds mainly on crustaceans, and averages about 3 lb (1.4 kg) in weight; larger specimens of up to 20 lb (9 kg) are becoming increasingly rare. The lake whitefish, together with the cisco (*Coregonus artedi*), the round whitefish (*Prosopium cylindraceum*), and the mountain whitefish (*Prosopium williamsoni*), is commercially important, as well as being a favorite among anglers.

Lake whitefish can be taken by fly-fishing with dry flies, and by spinning with artificial baits such as small, bright spinners and spoons. They can also be caught by float-fishing or bottom-fishing with natural baits, including cut fish.

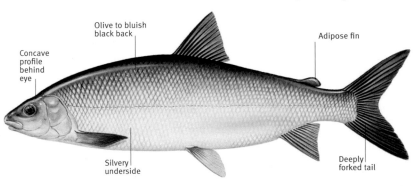

Olive to bluish black back

Adipose fin

Concave profile behind eye

Silvery underside

Deeply forked tail

Lepomis macrochirus (freshwater)

Bluegill

WEIGHT Up to 4 lb (1.8 kg).

TYPES OF WATER Quiet, reedy waters.

DISTRIBUTION From the Great Lakes to the Gulf of Mexico and New Mexico; introduced elsewhere.

FISHING METHODS Very light tackle, bait-, lure-, and fly-fishing.

A small relative of the black bass, the bluegill is one of the most widely distributed panfish, and probably the most fished-for species in North America. Panfish, which also include crappies, sunfish, and pumpkinseed (see pp.134–35), are fish that are too small to be considered true gamefish, but yet still provide good angling and eating.

The bluegill averages 4 oz (113 g), but large specimens can weigh around 4 lb (1.8 kg). Use small minnows, worms, maggots, and jigs for float-fishing; miniature spinners and crankbaits for baitcasting; and tiny wet flies, nymphs, and dry flies for fly-fishing.

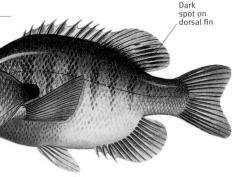

Dark spot on dorsal fin

Lepomis cyanellus (freshwater)

Green sunfish

WEIGHT Up to 2¼ lb (1 kg).
TYPES OF WATER Streams, rivers, lakes, and ponds.
DISTRIBUTION From the Great Lakes to Texas.
FISHING METHODS Very light tackle, bait-, lure-, and fly-fishing.

The *Lepomis* genus is part of the Centrarchidae family of sunfish. These ray-finned fish are widely distributed in streams, rivers, and lakes throughout the United States and Canada. Many of these are taken as panfish by anglers, and they are often bred to stock lakes.

The green sunfish is one of the most common *Lepomis* sunfish. Like other species in this genus, the green sunfish has elongated gill covers, or opercular flaps, which have an earlike appearance, which is why these fish are also known as eared sunfish. The green sunfish has a more elongated body than most other *Lepomis* species, and the upper jaw of its large mouth extends back to below the midpoint of the eye.

This fish is primarily a stream-dweller, but it may also be found in stillwaters. It inhabits vegetated areas in clear to turbid water with little or no current. The green sunfish is a very versatile fish that is able to tolerate a wide range of environmental conditions; because of this, it is often the first sunfish species to repopulate depleted areas.

GILL COVERS

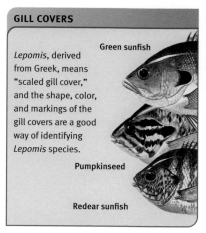

Lepomis, derived from Greek, means "scaled gill cover," and the shape, color, and markings of the gill covers are a good way of identifying *Lepomis* species.

Green sunfish

Pumpkinseed

Redear sunfish

Angling techniques for green sunfish fish are similar to those used to catch bluegill (*see* p.133) and crappies (*right*). Although their relatively small size makes them barely suitable as pan-fish, they are popular with anglers, since they tend to attack almost any bait and will usually put up a tough fight.

Other notable *Lepomis* species include the bluegill, the redear sunfish (*Lepomis microlophus*)—known as the "shellcraker" because it crushes snails and clams with its powerful, grinding teeth—and the redbreast sunfish (*Lepomis auritus*), which is most abundant in the creeks and medium-sized rivers of the Atlantic slope. The attractive pumpkinseed (*Lepomis gibbosus*) is a little fish that lives among the weeds in lakes, ponds, and quiet river pools.

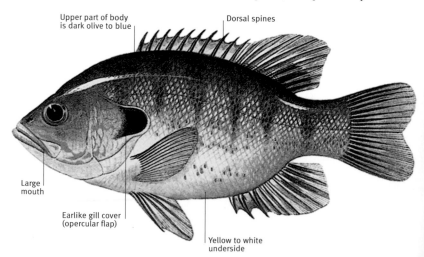

Upper part of body is dark olive to blue

Dorsal spines

Large mouth

Earlike gill cover (opercular flap)

Yellow to white underside

Pomoxis nigromaculatus (freshwater)

Black crappie

WEIGHT Up to 6 lb (2.75 kg).

TYPES OF WATER Ponds, rivers, and lakes.

DISTRIBUTION Eastern North America, from southern Canada to the Gulf of mexico; introduced elsewhere.

FISHING METHODS Very light tackle, bait-, lure-, and fly-fishing.

The black crappie and its close relative the white crappie (*Pomoxis annularis*) are very popular fish in parts of the United States, both for sport and for eating. The black crappie tends to be bigger than the white crappie, but neither species grows to a particularly large size. The overall coloration is usually darker in the black crappie, but the most reliable way to distinguish between the two is to count the spines in the first dorsal fin: the black crappie has seven or eight, while the white crappie has six.

These two species are relatives of the black bass family, which includes largemouth and smallmouth bass (*see* p.123). Crappies are generally found in the same kinds of waters, such as ponds, rivers, and lakes. Although they often occur together, the black crappie thrives better in slightly clearer water than the white crappie. Crappies tend to school around weed beds and over mud or sand, and feed on small insect larvae and crustaceans. Larger individuals will also eat small fish.

A favorite time to fish for crappies is when the water starts to warm up during the spring. These fish spawn when the water reaches around 52°F (11°C), but just before spawning, when the temperature of the water is 48–51°F (9–10°C), they move into shallow water and feed voraciously. Crappies are often found in coves, around rocks, and among sunken trees. Fishing with small jigs is a popular strategy.

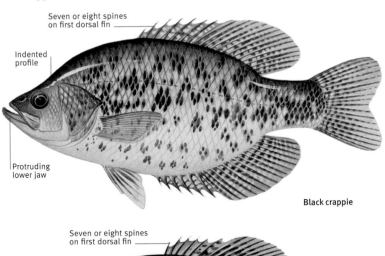

Seven or eight spines on first dorsal fin

Indented profile

Protruding lower jaw

Black crappie

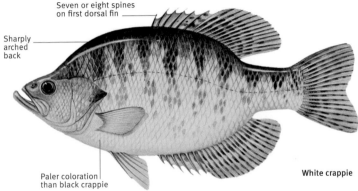

Seven or eight spines on first dorsal fin

Sharply arched back

Paler coloration than black crappie

White crappie

Oncorhynchus tshawytscha (freshwater)

Chinook salmon

WEIGHT Up to 135 lb (60 kg).

TYPES OF WATER Rivers, lakes, and oceans.

DISTRIBUTION Arctic Ocean and north Pacific Ocean and the rivers that flow into them.

FISHING METHODS Trolling (offshore and estuaries); lure- and fly-fishing (rivers).

These highly prized game fish are also known as king salmon. Chinook are the largest Pacific salmon, and they are immensely hard-fighting, powerful fish. Like all salmon, they begin their lives in freshwater. Chinook salmon fry can migrate to sea when they are only three months old, but generally they remain in the spawning rivers for one to three years before migrating to the oceans, where they feed and mature. These salmon can migrate huge distances at sea; then they return to the rivers they were born in, spawn once, and die. Adult chinook in the oceans are dark green to blue-black on the head and back, and silvery underneath. As they migrate inland, the breeding colors appear, with tinges of brownish reds and purples.

MIGRATING SALMON SHOAL
At times, the cold waters of the Alaska rivers are filled with dense, migrating schools of chinook salmon. These large numbers of fish, intent on reaching their spawning ground, are easy prey for large mammals, such as bears.

OFFSHORE TROLLING

Chinook salmon are among several Pacific salmon species that are successfully caught when feeding in the ocean, prior to returning to rivers for spawning. Anglers take them by trolling just offshore and in the estuaries, as the fish return. They can be caught in large numbers when big schools are found. Like virtually all salmon, chinook do not feed when they enter river systems, so the river angler must induce the salmon to take lures or flies when they would not do so naturally.

TYPES OF CHINOOK

There are two types of Chinook salmon: the "stream type," found mostly in the headwaters of larger river systems, and the "ocean type," found mostly in coastal streams and rivers. Stream-type chinook spend a long time in freshwater, whereas those of the ocean type often remain in freshwater for only a year before migrating to the ocean. During their ocean-living phase, ocean-type chinook salmon usually remain in coastal waters.

Dark greenish blue coloration on head

Straight lateral line

Dark spots on tail fin

Oncorhynchus kisutch (freshwater)

Coho salmon

WEIGHT Up to 33 lb (15 kg).

TYPES OF WATER Rivers, lakes, oceans.

DISTRIBUTION North Pacific Ocean and the rivers that flow into it.

FISHING METHODS Trolling with lures (offshore); spinning and fly-fishing (rivers).

The coho salmon is an extremely important game species to anglers. At sea, coho salmon are a dark metallic blue-green with small black spots on the upper sides, and silver paling to white underneath. When running inland for the spawning season, the fish turn bright green on the head and back, red on the sides, and dark underneath.

Young coho salmon will usually spend one to two years in their spawning rivers and then migrate at night either to the sea or to lakes. Here they feed on plankton, crustaceans, small fish, and jellyfish. Some never leave the freshwater lakes and, while they may be sexually mature, they never spawn. Like all Pacific salmon, coho return to the river in which they were born to breed and then die after spawning. In rivers, coho salmon do not tend to mix with the more aggressive salmon species like the chum and the chinook (*opposite*).

A PRIZED QUARRY

Coho salmon are renowned for being very hard-fighting fish and, while not as large as the chinook salmon, they are nevertheless a highly prized quarry. Inland, they are caught by spinning and fly-fishing. Fly anglers, especially, look for slower-moving waters in which to fish for this species. At sea, anglers catch coho salmon mainly by trolling, using downriggers and lures.

Pale gum line of lower jaw

Dark spots on upper part of tail fin

COHO SALMON FISHING
Anglers fish from boats in the waters of Giltoyees River, Douglas Channel, British Columbia, as the coho salmon run in from the Pacific.

Gadus morhua (saltwater)

Atlantic cod

WEIGHT Up to 210 lb (96 kg).

TYPES OF WATER Temperate and cold waters, from shoreline to continental shelf.

DISTRIBUTION North Atlantic Ocean.

FISHING METHODS Bait- and lure-fishing.

Subject to intense commercial pressure for centuries, the Atlantic cod stocks of Britain, Greenland, and Newfoundland are close to total collapse; only rigorously enforced conservation methods will ensure the long-term survival of this species. However, in some places it is still possible to enjoy sport fishing for large cod, both from boats and from the shore. Cod can grow up to 6½ ft (2 m) long. Their coloration can vary from brown to green or gray on the back, paling to white or silver underneath.

WIDE-RANGING AND OMNIVOROUS

Atlantic cod inhabit a wide range of habitats, including estuaries, inshore waters, wrecks, reefs, and deepwater fjords, right out to the edge of the continental shelf. They are most likely to come close inshore during rough seas. Atlantic cod are voracious feeders, eating everything from weed and invertebrates to small fish, even including the young of their own species. They school in large numbers, close to the bottom. They are caught mainly on baits and lures (jigs, pirks, or shads) fished from the bottom to mid-waters, but they can also be caught using big flies close to the sea bed.

White lateral line

Single barbel

Square-ended tail

SHOALING ATLANTIC COD
Atlantic cod are a favorite fish for sport and for the table. Although they can grow to very large sizes, they often come close inshore, where they can be targeted by anglers from the beach or rocks, or from boats.

Red drum

WEIGHT Up to 100 lb (45 kg).

TYPES OF WATER Coastal waters and estuaries.

DISTRIBUTION West-central Atlantic Ocean.

FISHING METHODS Bait-, lure-, and fly-fishing from boats or the shore.

The red drum, also called redfish, channel bass, or "croaker" (*see below*), is one of the most important sport-fishing species in the southern United States. Red drum

may grow to about 5 ft (1.5 m) in length, although most are much smaller. They have an overall red coloration, with one or more dark spots at the base of the tail.

Red drum are found predominantly in coastal waters and estuaries, mostly over sand and muddy bottoms. They prefer to feed in the surf zone, mainly on mollusks, crustaceans, and small fish. When red drum move into shallow and clear water on saltwater flats, it may be possible to sight-fish for them, and here they give excellent sport. In shallow water it is important to approach quietly, as red drum spook easily.

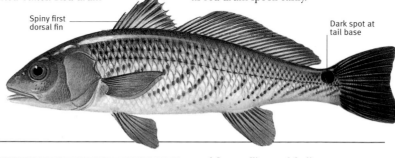

Spiny first dorsal fin

Dark spot at tail base

Black drum

WEIGHT Up to 110 lb (50 kg).

TYPES OF WATER Coastal waters and estuaries.

DISTRIBUTION Western Atlantic Ocean, from Nova Scotia to Argentina, including the Caribbean.

FISHING METHODS Bait fishing from shore, piers, or boats.

The black drum is a broad, chunky-looking fish with a tall back, and plenty of distinctive barbels under the lower jaw,

used for smelling and feeling out prey. The adult black drum has a white underside, but the overall coloration varies from light gray through to almost bronze. The four or five dark vertical bars on the flank disappear with age.

Both black and red drum (*see above*) are often called "croakers" because of their ability to make croaking (or drumming) sounds via an air bladder. Black drum are best at doing this, and anglers can sometimes hear passing shoals because of these sounds. Texas is a favored place to fish for large black drum, especially during February and March, when they gather for spawning.

Broad dark stripes

Blunt-shaped tail fin

Chin barbels

Centropomus undecimalis (saltwater)

Common snook

WEIGHT Up to 50 lb (24 kg).

TYPES OF WATER Warm inshore waters, lagoons, and estuaries.

DISTRIBUTION Western and southwestern Atlantic Ocean; Caribbean.

FISHING METHODS Bait-, lure-, and fly-fishing.

The common snook is the most abundant of the various snook species. This species has a long snout and a lower jaw that extends farther than the upper one. Its coloration is dark on its back, silver on its sides, and white underneath. There is a distinctive black lateral stripe that extends well into the broad, forked tail fin.

Common snook are found in inshore coastal waters, lagoons, and estuaries, usually at a depth of less than 70 ft (20 m). They do not tolerate cold water and their range is determined by the water temperature. They can tolerate freshwater and feed mainly on small fish, shrimp, and small crabs. This species responds to angling with baits, lures, and flies.

Sharp gill covers

Black lateral stripe

Trachinotus falcatus (saltwater)

Permit

WEIGHT Up to 80 lb (36 kg).

TYPES OF WATER Subtropical coastal shallows and reefs.

DISTRIBUTION Western Atlantic Ocean from Massachusetts Bay to southeastern Brazil, including the Bahamas and much of the Caribbean.

FISHING METHODS Fly- and bait-fishing.

Permit grow to 4 ft (1.2 m) long, and are deep-bodied, with a distinctive, crescent-shaped tail fin and an orange-yellow patch on the abdomen. They frequent shallow, coastal waters, feeding on various types of crustaceans. Famous

INDO-PACIFIC PERMIT

Although not quite as large as its American cousin, the Indo-Pacific permit (*Trachinotus blochi*) is a popular fishing quarry in parts of northern Australia and the Indian Ocean islands, such as the Seychelles.

areas for fishing this species include the Florida Keys, the Bahamas, Mexico, and Costa Rica. Fly-fishing on the flats is the classic way to catch them, although they are hard-fighting, wary, and often reluctant to take a fly. They also form schools around wrecks and reefs, where bait-fishing methods work well. Crabs are the favored bait.

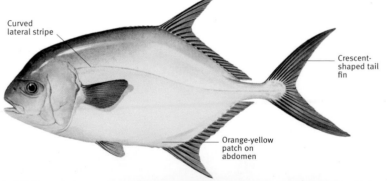

Curved lateral stripe

Crescent-shaped tail fin

Orange-yellow patch on abdomen

Morone saxatilis (saltwater)

Striped bass

WEIGHT Up to 125 lb (57 kg).

TYPES OF WATER Coastal waters; freshwater and brackish rivers.

DISTRIBUTION Western Atlantic Ocean.

FISHING METHODS Bait-, lure-, and fly-fishing.

The striped bass is an important saltwater sport-fishing species in North America. It is colored greenish gray above, becoming paler beneath, with six to nine dark horizontal stripes. Adult striped bass feed on fish and crustaceans, and they stop feeding before spawning. Although mainly a saltwater species, these large fish migrate into freshwater to spawn in the spring, and there are various fresh

and brackish water populations from Louisiana to Florida. When massed in schools, the elegant lines of striped bass are an attractive sight in clear waters.

One of fishing's success stories, striped bass were once commercially fished to dangerously low population levels, but their worth as sporting fish was officially recognized, and a radical conservation program was introduced with great success. The numbers of these hard-fighting fish have now been restored to a sustainable level.

When the fish are running, they often come close inshore and can be caught from boats and from the shore using a variety of angling methods. They respond well to bait- and lure-fishing, while fly anglers also enjoy great success when they come within casting range.

Six to nine stripes

Pale underside

Pseudopleuronectes americanus (saltwater)

Winter flounder

WEIGHT Up to 8 lb (4 kg).

TYPES OF WATER Soft to moderately hard bottoms in coastal waters.

DISTRIBUTION Western Atlantic Ocean from Labrador, Canada, to Georgia, US.

FISHING METHODS Bait- and lure-fishing.

The winter flounder is a popular game fish for anglers fishing the coastal waters of the eastern shores of North America. It occurs in waters from tidal shallows to a maximum depth of 400 ft (120 m). This fish is usually mainly brown in coloration, often with dark spots. A similar species, the European

flounder (*Platichthys flesus*), is found in coastal and brackish waters from western Europe to the Black Sea, and is often present in estuaries. Also a popular target for anglers, it is generally smaller than the winter flounder, reaching a maximum weight of 7 lb (3.25 kg).

Lateral line curved over pectoral fin

Dark spots

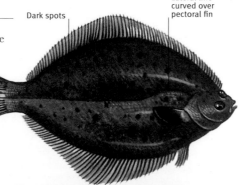

Coryphaena hippurus (saltwater)

Dorado

WEIGHT Up to 90 lb (40 kg).

TYPES OF WATER Tropical and subtropical open or coastal waters.

DISTRIBUTION Atlantic Ocean; Mediterranean; Indian Ocean; Pacific Ocean.

FISHING METHODS Bait-, lure-, and fly-fishing from boats.

Also known as mahi mahi, dolphinfish, or golden mackerel, dorado are among the fastest-growing fish in the sea, reaching 6 ft (2 m) in length and living for only about five years. Their green or electric-blue upper body, and gold sides flashed with green, seem to light up when the fish are hooked, showing

FEMALE HEAD SHAPE

Female dorado (known as cows), and the young of both sexes, tend to have a more softly rounded head than the males (*see below*). Mature male dorado, often known as bulls, are usually larger than the females and have a square forehead with a higher and flatter shape.

off neonlike colors during highly acrobatic fights. The dorsal fin runs the length of the body. Small dorados travel in schools; large adults travel alone or in pairs. Fishing is best near floating objects such as logs, reeds, or flotsam out at sea, as well as near weed lines and buoys, where they feed on plankton, crustaceans, small fish, and squid attracted to the shelter.

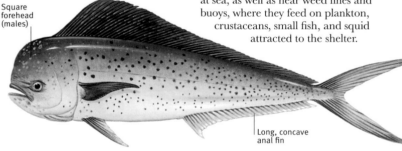

Square forehead (males)

Long, concave anal fin

Acanthocybium solandri (saltwater)

Wahoo

WEIGHT Up to 180 lb (83 kg).

TYPES OF WATER Tropical and subtropical waters.

DISTRIBUTION Atlantic Ocean; Mediterranean; Indian Ocean; Pacific Ocean.

FISHING METHODS Trolling from boats with baits and lures; occasionally drift-fishing with livebait.

Wahoo (called queenfish in the Caribbean and ono in Hawaii) are fast, powerful fish that can swim in short bursts at up to 60 mph (100 km/h).

Wahoo change direction quickly and jump repeatedly when hooked. They have a slim body shape not unlike the king mackerel, and plenty of very sharp teeth. The snout is long and tapers to a point, with the underside jaw slightly longer than the upper. The upper body is dark or electric blue with waved stripes along the flanks. Rows of small finlets lie directly behind the dorsal fins and the anal fin. Wahoo swim in waters of 70 to 86°F (21–30°C), usually preferring the waters around reefs with warm current lines and schools of baitfish, and large holes in the seabed.

Long, tapering jawline

Tail-end finlets

Blue-striped sides

Scomber scombrus (saltwater)

Atlantic mackerel

WEIGHT Up to 8 lb (3.5 kg).
TYPES OF WATER Seas and oceans.
DISTRIBUTION North Atlantic Ocean; North Sea; Mediterranean.
FISHING METHODS Bait-, lure-, and fly-fishing.

MACKEREL SPAWNING TIMES

Although genetically the same, the Atlantic mackerel populations in United States waters fall into two distinct groups: one spawns during April and May in the mid-Atlantic Bight, while the other spawns during June and July in the Gulf of St. Lawrence.

The Atlantic mackerel is important both as a sporting fish worth catching in its own right and as a baitfish that will attract larger fish. It can reach up to 2 ft (60 cm) in length and its upper parts are metallic green with 20 to 23 dark, wavy bars, while its underside is silvery.

The Atlantic mackerel forms large schools and feeds mainly on smaller fish near the surface. At times, these fish will drive small prey species to the surface in a feeding frenzy, making the sea appear to boil. Few saltwater species will not take mackerel bait; it can even be effective when angling in freshwater, such as when targeting pike.

Dark bars on back

Spots below lateral line

Scomberomorus cavalla (saltwater)

King mackerel

WEIGHT Up to 100 lb (45 kg).
TYPES OF WATER Seas and oceans, offshore and inshore waters.
DISTRIBUTION Atlantic Ocean.
FISHING METHOD Bait-, lure-, and fly-fishing.

Also known as kingfish, the king mackerel is a hugely popular sporting fish. In the US, small king mackerel under 15 lb (6.8 kg) are often referred to as "snakes," and larger specimens over 30 lb (13.5 kg) are nicknamed "smokers" for their speed and ability to "smoke" line from a reel when hooked. The king

mackerel has a blue-green back, silvery sides, and a tapered, strongly streamlined body and tail. The lateral line curves suddenly downward after the second dorsal fin. This species feeds on smaller fish, shrimp, and squid.

FISHING APPROACHES

In the US, slow trolling with livebaits—porgie, also known as menhaden, is a popular choice—or with lures is the best fishing method for this species, but in other areas of the world they are also caught with flies. King mackerel are caught predominantly in offshore and inshore waters. There are numerous professional king mackerel fishing tournaments held in the US.

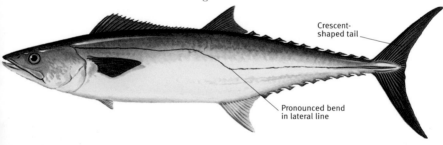

Crescent-shaped tail

Pronounced bend in lateral line

Lutjanus cyanopterus (saltwater)

Cubera snapper

WEIGHT Up to 125 lb (57 kg).

TYPES OF WATER Coastal waters.

DISTRIBUTION Western central and southwestern Atlantic; Caribbean.

FISHING METHODS Bait-, lure-, and fly-fishing.

Cubera snapper are said to be the largest species of snapper. Their coloration is dark brown to gray, sometimes with a reddish tinge overall. They have very strong teeth—one pair of canines is particularly large and is visible when the mouth is closed.

Adult cubera snapper tend to be found offshore around rocky ledges and reefs, in depths up to about 165 ft (50 m). The young sometimes inhabit estuaries, areas of extensive mangroves, and grass beds. Cubera snapper feed mainly on a variety of smaller fish as well as shrimp and crabs.

FISHING FOR CUBERAS

At full moon during July and August in southern Florida, adult cubera snappers move up from deep water to depths of around 200 ft (60 m) to spawn. This is the best time to fish for big specimens. Use powerful tackle in these depths, as the fish always try to head for the safety of the rocks.

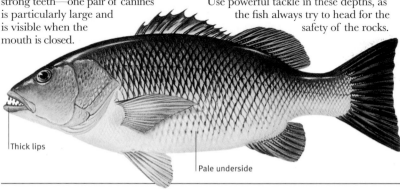

Thick lips

Pale underside

Ocyurus chrysurus (saltwater)

Yellowtail snapper

WEIGHT Up to 8¾ lb (4 kg).

TYPES OF WATER Coastal waters, coral reefs.

DISTRIBUTION Western Atlantic Ocean (Massachusetts to Brazil); Caribbean.

FISHING METHODS Bait-, lure-, and fly-fishing.

Yellowtails are fairly small among snappers. They have distinctive yellow spots on the upper side, with olive to bluish coloration, blending down to pink and yellow stripes. A broad lateral yellow stripe runs from the mouth to the tail.

Yellowtail snapper are found mainly in coastal

waters where they school and spawn, mainly during summer. They are heavily fished for over grass beds and reefs, and offshore, where they frequent sandy patches that lie around reefs.

CATCHING YELLOWTAILS

Like various other snapper species, yellowtails respond well to baits and lures, and can also be taken by fly-fishing. A noted way to attract these snappers is to put out a net of chum. They are often voracious feeders and can be easy to catch when they are feeding hard. The southeastern parts of Florida, and especially the Keys, are the best places to catch large numbers of yellowtail snappers.

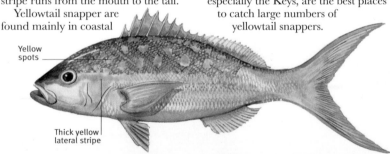

Yellow spots

Thick yellow lateral stripe

Lutjanus analis (saltwater)

Mutton snapper

WEIGHT Up to 35 lb (15.5 kg).

TYPES OF WATER Clear, rocky coastal waters; continental shelf.

DISTRIBUTION Western Atlantic Ocean; Caribbean.

FISHING METHOD Bait-, lure-, and fly-fishing.

The brightly colored mutton snapper is one of the most numerous snappers to be found anywhere in the Caribbean or the coastal waters surrounding southern Florida. Coloration on the upper sides is an olive green that blends into a whitish lower side and belly, with a slight red tinge. A black spot lies on the upper back area just above the lateral line. A pair of striking blue stripes run on each side of the cheek area of the fish. Bars on the body of the mutton snapper are prominent when the fish is resting; the body color becomes plainer when the fish is swimming.

INSHORE WATERS

Mutton snapper are usually found inshore around grass beds, mangroves, and in tidal creeks, and sometimes larger individuals are caught offshore.

Mutton snapper are sometimes mistaken for the lane snapper (*Lutjanus synagris*), a somewhat similar species, and are often marketed as "red" snapper.

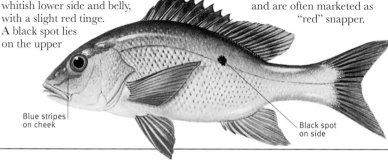

Blue stripes on cheek

Black spot on side

Rachycentron canadum (saltwater)

Cobia

WEIGHT Up to 150 lb (68 kg).

TYPES OF WATER Warm, coastal waters.

DISTRIBUTION Atlantic Ocean; Indian Ocean; Pacific Ocean.

FISHING METHODS Bait- and lure-fishing from boats.

A cobia has a long, slim body with a broad, slightly depressed head, and a protruding lower jaw. Its overall coloration is dark brown with a strong dark lateral stripe that runs from the eye to the tail. The distinctive first dorsal fin has seven to nine spines that do not have any membrane connecting them. The cobia is a powerful fish that can grow up to 6½ ft (2 m) in length, and is highly migratory, preferring warm water. Often this species can be seen traveling in shallow water, around buoys, anchored boats, and navigation markers. They feed on small fish and crustaceans.

SIGHT-FISHING IN FLORIDA

The cobia is a hugely popular sporting species, especially in the waters off Florida. Large numbers spend the winter months on Florida's Atlantic coast around the reefs and wrecks. Sight-fishing for them is exciting. The angler must cast lures in front of a moving cobia and then retrieve it across its path. Cobia are famous for accompanying other large fish, especially rays, and many anglers will look for these when targeting cobia.

Membrane-free dorsal fin

Prominent lateral stripe

Large anal fin

Caranx hippos (saltwater)

Crevalle jack

WEIGHT Up to 70 lb (32 kg).

TYPES OF WATER Warm coastal waters, brackish estuaries.

DISTRIBUTION Western and eastern Atlantic Ocean; western Mediterranean.

FISHING METHODS Bait-, lure-, and fly-fishing from boats and shore.

The crevalle jack is dark greenish blue on the back, with silvery or brassy sides. It has dark spots on the edge of the gill covers and near the pectoral fins, with sometimes a third spot farther back. This fish can reach 4 ft (1.2 m) in length, though inshore specimens are much smaller. It can swim up river systems, and the young inhabit inshore areas. The crevalle jack is an aggressive fish, able to battle hard for long periods. It is often attracted to boats by chumming, and may make unusual grunting sounds when caught.

RUTHLESS KILLERS

Crevalle jacks are experts at working around schools of baitfish and then smashing into them. When this happens near or on the surface, it can be a spectacular sight. Waves of jacks attacking their prey sound almost like a washing-machine in its spin cycle.

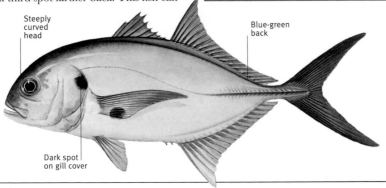

Steeply curved head

Blue-green back

Dark spot on gill cover

Caranx latus (saltwater)

Horse-eye jack

WEIGHT Up to 30 lb (13.5 kg).

TYPES OF WATER Offshore reefs; sometimes fresh or brackish water.

DISTRIBUTION Western and eastern Atlantic Ocean.

FISHING METHODS Bait-, lure-, and fly-fishing from boats and shore.

Sometimes also known as "big-eye" jacks, horse-eye jacks are similar to crevalle jacks, with which they sometimes school, but they have large eyes and do not grow as big—reaching a maximum length of about 3¼ ft (1 m). Overall, their coloration is gray to blue on the back and silver to white on the belly; the tail fin is a distinctive yellow, and the top part of the rear dorsal fin is almost black. What distinguishes them from crevalle jacks are the small scales on the chest area and the absence of a dark blotch on the pectoral fin. There is sometimes a small dark patch near the gill cover.

Horse-eye jacks feed mainly on other fish, shrimp, and invertebrates, and they gather in large schools. Like crevalle jacks, waves of them hitting smaller fish can often be seen from a distance.

Large eye

Yellow tail fin

Seriola dumerili (saltwater)

Greater amberjack

WEIGHT Up to 175 lb (80 kg).

TYPES OF WATER Warm, deep water.

DISTRIBUTION Atlantic Ocean, Indian Ocean, and Pacific Ocean; Mediterranean.

FISHING METHODS Bait-, lure-, and fly-fishing from boats.

Greater amberjacks are generally silvery in color, but darker on the back. There is a stripe that runs along each side. Both males and females grow at the same rate, but male amberjacks do not survive much beyond seven years old, so the largest specimens are nearly all females. Smaller amberjacks can easily be confused with other jack species.

Greater amberjacks spend much of their time relatively close to the surface, and they tend to swim either singly or in small groups, preferring to inhabit reefs and wrecks in warm, deep waters, where they feed on smaller fish. Amberjacks are aggressive predators that are difficult fish to land successfully. They fight hard, run savagely, and often crash-dive repeatedly in their attempts to fight off an angler.

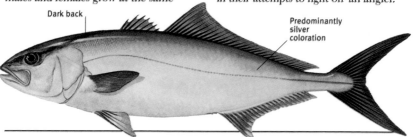

Dark back

Predominantly silver coloration

Seriola lalandi (saltwater)

California yellowtail

WEIGHT Up to 215 lb (97 kg).

TYPES OF WATER Warmish waters near the shore or beyond the continental shelf.

DISTRIBUTION Southwestern and southeastern Atlantic Ocean; Indian Ocean; Pacific Ocean.

FISHING METHODS Lure- and bait-fishing from boats or shore.

Also known as yellowtail amberjack or yellowtail kingfish, California yellowtails are powerful fish that inhabit the upper waters of the open sea. They grow up to 8 ft (2.5 m) in length. Coloration varies, but usually they are dark green or blue on the back, shading to a metallic blue-green on the sides and silver or white on the

YELLOWTAIL JIGGING

Yellowtails respond well to jigging in water up to about 200 ft (60 m) deep. Drop the jig to the bottom, and then retrieve it quickly—this called butterfly or vertical jigging (*see* pp.88–89). Wind as fast as you can, for a yellowtail will hit the jig with ease if it chooses to. When yellowtails are feeding on squid, they do so exclusively and will touch nothing else. Live squid is the perfect bait in this situation.

belly. The tail is bright yellow, and there is a yellow or gold stripe on the flank.

Small yellowtails often form large schools close to coasts, but larger fish tend to form small groups around deepwater reefs and offshore islands. They prefer clean water with a temperature of more than 64°F (18°C). Yellowtails are fished for mainly with lures and baits.

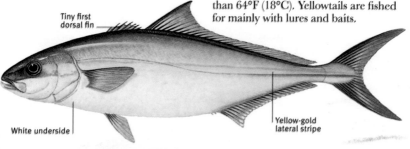

Tiny first dorsal fin

White underside

Yellow-gold lateral stripe

Albula vulpes (saltwater)

Bonefish

WEIGHT Up to 22 lb (10 kg).
TYPES OF WATER Shallow waters with a sandy or muddy bottom.
DISTRIBUTION Worldwide in warm seas and oceans.
FISHING METHODS Fly-fishing and bait-fishing.

Arguably the most popular saltwater fly-fishing quarry, the bonefish is of little value commercially as a food fish. Nevertheless, this species is a highly prized sight-fishing quarry of the flats.

The bonefish is silvery gray in coloration, with darker vertical bars that fade with age. The fins are darker than the body. It has a slim, elongated shape that enables it to feed close to the bottom in shallow water, where it seeks out crustaceans and shrimp. These fish can often be seen feeding with their tails sticking out of the water as they burrow down in the mud and sand to root out food. Anglers call this "tailing," and it is one of the classic sights of tropical fishing on saltwater flats.

Bonefish are hard-fighting fish and can run fast when hooked. They can be taken on various baits, especially shrimp or prawns, and on small jigs. Larger specimens are usually taken on bait in deep water. However, fly-fishing on the flats is the classic method.

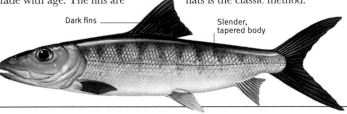

Dark fins

Slender, tapered body

Pomatomus saltatrix (saltwater)

Bluefish

WEIGHT Up to 32 lb (14.5 kg).
TYPES OF WATER Coastal surf or moving water, near beaches and headlands.
DISTRIBUTION All oceans except the eastern and northwestern Pacific Ocean.
FISHING METHODS Bait-, lure-, and fly-fishing.

The bluefish has a greenish gray back and sides and a silvery underside. This highly migratory species tends to move to warmer waters during the winter and then cooler waters in summer. It is most often found behind the breakers on surf beaches, in the surf itself, and around rocky headlands where there is clean saltwater and a good supply of smaller fish for food. The bluefish has extremely sharp teeth, which makes the use of wire traces (*see* p.33) advisable. Be careful of the teeth when unhooking this fish.

FEEDING FRENZY

One of the most effective ways to find bluefish is to look for schools of their preferred prey, or baitfish, such as mullet and menhaden. Hungry bluefish will signal their presence by smashing into the baitfish on the surface. Schools of bluefish may attack smaller fish in shallow water, in a feeding frenzy. These fish are famous for forming large schools. One school seen in Narragansett Bay, Rhode Island, in 1901 was estimated to be 4 to 5 miles (6–8 km) long.

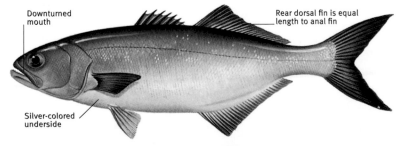

Downturned mouth

Rear dorsal fin is equal length to anal fin

Silver-colored underside

Yellowfin tuna

WEIGHT Up to 440 lb (200 kg).
TYPES OF WATER Ocean.
DISTRIBUTION Atlantic, Indian, and Pacific oceans.
FISHING METHOD Bait-, lure-, and fly-fishing from boats.

The yellowfin tuna is dark and metallic-looking on the back, blending into yellow on the sides, and a silvery color on the belly. The dorsal and anal fins are bright yellow. This is a highly migratory species of tuna that is usually found in water no more than 330 ft (100 m) deep. It tends to congregate in large schools. Yellowfin tuna often school with other fish species of a similar size rather than specifically with members of their own species. They commonly mix with other species of tuna and, in the eastern Pacific, with dolphins. They feed mainly on fish, squid, and crustaceans.

The yellowfin is an immensely important sporting species and is known for being hard-fighting. Bait- and lure-fishing are the most common fishing methods, but some anglers manage to catch large yellowfins on heavy-duty fly-fishing gear.

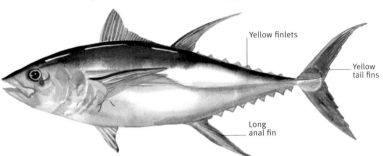

Yellow finlets

Yellow tail fins

Long anal fin

Atlantic bonito

WEIGHT Up to 25 lb (11 kg).
TYPES OF WATER Ocean.
DISTRIBUTION Atlantic Ocean; Mediterranean; western Indian Ocean.
FISHING METHODS Bait-, lure-, and fly-fishing from boats.

The Atlantic bonito has a typical tuna shape, but differs slightly from the similar-looking Pacific bonito (*Sarda chilensis*). The side stripes of the Atlantic species run diagonally and there are 20 to 23 spines on the first dorsal fin, whereas the Pacific bonito has 17 to 19 spines on its first dorsal fin. The Atlantic bonito is primarily a deepwater fish. It requires a sea temperature of 59 to 72°F (15–22°C), and feeds on shrimp, small fish, and squid. It can be cannibalistic.

This species can be successfully targeted with light tackle. While trolling works well, it is also fun to cast lures and flies at them when the schools are feeding on small fish near or at the surface. It is best to position your boat upwind or uptide of the school and quietly drift down toward the fish. The bonito is known for hesitating when first hooked, but within a few seconds it is likely to charge off at high speed.

Striped upper parts

Large mouth

Great barracuda

WEIGHT Up to 110 lb (50 kg).

TYPES OF WATER Tropical waters.

DISTRIBUTION Atlantic Ocean, Indian Ocean, and Pacific Ocean.

FISHING METHODS Bait- and lure-fishing from boats or shore.

The large mouth of this predatory fish is lined with razor-sharp teeth. The upper body is bluish gray, blending into green and then silver or white on the belly. There are 18 to 23 dark bars on the upper body, and black spots below the lateral line.

The great barracuda can be found close to inshore coral reefs, seagrass, and mangroves, and even near structures such as piers and jetties. Larger specimens also live in the open ocean, where they often remain near the surface. Barracuda sometimes form schools, but generally they are solitary fish.

FEEDING HABITS

The great barracuda is an aggressive feeder that often charges into schools of baitfish, using its large teeth to slash at its prey. The injured and dead fish are then consumed. Avoid wearing anything shiny when swimming in waters inhabited by great barracuda, as the fish are attracted to this visual stimulus and have been known to attack. Anglers can target this species with lures and livebaits, either from boats or the shore.

Sharp spines on dorsal fin

Pale tail fin tips

Dark spots

Sailfish

WEIGHT Up to 220 lb (100 kg).

TYPES OF WATER Temperate and tropical coastal waters.

DISTRIBUTION Atlantic Ocean, Indian Ocean, and Pacific Ocean.

FISHING METHODS Trolling with baits and lures; fly-fishing.

With its long bill and sail-like spotted dorsal fin, the sailfish is unmistakable. It also has very long and narrow pelvic fins. The upper parts are blue-black, while the underside is silvery white. There are about 20 pale blue, vertical bars along the flanks. This migratory, oceanic species is found in greatest numbers close to the coast, often in large schools. Sailfish feed predominantly on smaller fish, squid, and crustaceans. Although sailfish do not grow as large as other billfish, they are exciting to catch.

FISHING METHODS

Sailfish can be targeted with light tackle by trolling from boats, with baits and lures. Kites are often used to spread out the lures behind the boat. Teasing fish in with livebait and then casting flies at them is also a popular technique for catching this species in some places. Off the Florida coast, where it is common practice to return all sailfish alive, anglers often fish mainly with livebaits. The waters off the Florida Keys are among the best for fishing sailfish.

Sail-like first dorsal fin

Long bill

Megalops atlanticus (saltwater)

Tarpon

WEIGHT Up to 355 lb (160 kg).

TYPES OF WATER Coastal waters, estuaries, lagoons, brackish rivers.

DISTRIBUTION Eastern and western Atlantic Ocean; Gulf of Mexico; Caribbean.

FISHING METHODS Bait-, lure-, and fly-fishing.

Tarpon offer great fishing in many different areas of the world. They look somewhat like oversized herring, but tarpon are actually closely related to eels. They have distinctive upturned mouths and bright, metallic, very hard scales.

Tarpon spawn in the open sea but they shoal and feed in shallower water, taking small fish and crustaceans. They are usually caught in estuaries, lagoons, tidal flats, mangrove swamps, and around structures, such as road bridges.

Tarpon are successfully fished with fish and crab baits, as well as with lures in some areas. When on tidal flats they are a popular target for accomplished fly-anglers. Tarpon can grow very large, and they are difficult to hook due to their bony mouths. These hard-fighting adversaries may leap several times in their efforts to shed the hook.

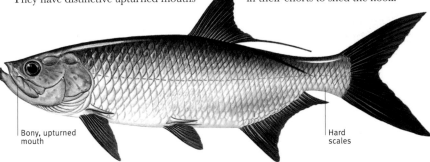

Bony, upturned mouth

Hard scales

Tetrapturus albidus (saltwater)

White marlin

WEIGHT Up to 180 lb (82 kg).

TYPES OF WATER Warm waters.

DISTRIBUTION Atlantic Ocean; Caribbean; Mediterranean.

FISHING METHODS Trolling with lures and baits; and fly-fishing.

White marlin are smaller than other marlin species, reaching only 10 ft (3 m) in length. Their body color varies from dark blue to dark brown on top, fading down to a silvery white underbelly. There are spots on the large dorsal fin, and the tips of the first dorsal, pectoral, and anal fins are rounded. The flanks may have rows of rather indistinct, whitish stripes. White marlin are found offshore in the Atlantic, Gulf of Mexico, and Caribbean, moving to higher latitudes as the waters warm with the seasons. They feed on squid and smaller open-water fish.

Trolling from big-game boats is the normal fishing method, but white marlin are fine quarry for light-tackle anglers, and can be fished for effectively with lures, baitfish, and flies when the fish are teased close to the boat. They tend to stay close to schools of baitfish, and structural areas such as reefs and canyons offer the best chances of making a catch.

Dark spots on dorsal fin

White stripes

Silvery white underside

Glossary

Adipose fin A small fin between the *dorsal fin* and the *caudal fin*.

AFTM/AFTMA The American Fishing Tackle Manufacturers' Association. AFTM numbers are codes for matching fly rods and fly lines. The AFTM scale is based on the weight of the first 30 ft (9.1 m) of the fly line. Manufacturers match rods to the weight of line that they can *cast* effectively. Reels are often described as being suitable for certain AFTM numbers.

Anadromous Fish species that are born in freshwater, migrate to saltwater, and then migrate back to freshwater to spawn.

Anal fin The fin located behind the anus.

Back-cast The part of the *cast* when both rod and line are behind the person who is casting.

Backing Thin line that is put on a reel (usually a fly reel) to increase the diameter of the *spool*.

Bait Natural or processed food (including *dead bait* and *livebait*) put on a hook to attract fish.

Baitfish Any small fish used for bait.

Bale arm The part of a *spinning reel* that guides the line on to the *spool*.

Barbel A barbule, or slender spine or bristle, located around the mouth or head of a fish.

Bluewater The deep waters of open oceans.

Brackish water Slightly salty water, such as in places where rivers run into the sea.

Braid Low-diameter, low-stretch fishing line, made by braiding together several strands of synthetic fiber.

Breaking strain The amount of dead-weight it takes to break a line, usually quoted in pounds (lb) or kilograms (kg).

Butt pad A protective pad with a fitting that holds the butt of a rod while fighting a fish, usually worn around the groin or lower stomach.

Caddis fly Aquatic insects that the flies used by fly-anglers are designed to imitate.

Cast To put a *lure*, *bait*, or imitation fly out on to the water, using a rod and reel.

Casting arc The path that a fly rod travels during the *cast*. Instructors often describe the parts of the arc in terms of the hands of a clock.

Caudal fin Tail fin.

Chum Chopped fish and other attractors, such as fish oil, put overboard to attract fish when sea-fishing from boats; also called "rubby dubby."

Clutch The *drag* system on a reel.

Conventional reel A reel with a revolving *spool* that multiplies leverage on the line as it is winched in; also called a baitcasting reel.

Dead bait Any dead fish or creature that is used for fishing bait.

Dead drift To fish a fly so that it drifts freely and travels at the same speed as the current.

Dorsal fin The fin located on the back of a fish, in front of the *adipose fin*.

Double-haul A fly-fishing technique that is used to increase line speed.

Downrigger A device on a boat that uses a cable and a weight to *troll* baits and lures at a set depth.

Drag The pressure applied internally to the *spool* of a reel, to make it harder work and thus more tiring for a fish to take line when running.

Dropoff A sudden drop in water depth.

Dry fly A fly that floats on top of the water.

Ebb tide The outgoing, or falling, tide.

Eddy (back eddy) A water current, or drift, that is moving in the opposite direction of the main current or flow.

Flasher board A reflective or colored board tied in front of a *bait* or *lure* for extra movement and additional visual attraction.

Flats Shallow, generally tidal, inshore saltwater areas that are waded by anglers.

Floating fly line A fly line made of material that floats on the surface of the water.

Flood tide The incoming, or rising, tide.

Forward cast The part of the *cast* when the line is in front of the person casting.

Freelining Fishing with baits but with no weights, allowing the bait to drift or swim naturally.

Fry A fish in an early stage of development, especially salmon or trout species.

Game fish Sometimes also referred to as *sport fish*, any freshwater and saltwater species of fish that is governed by sport-fishing laws.

Gills Vascular organs on a fish, used for aquatic respiration.

Gravel guard Either a separate neoprene wrap worn around the ankles, or the part of a pair of waders that clips on to the wading boot, to stop gravel from getting into boots.

Grilse A young Atlantic salmon that has returned to the river from the sea, to *spawn* for the first time.

Gully A channel formed by moving water.

Indicator A means by which anglers can visually detect a fish bite—often a float or a small, visible floating object secured to the end of the fly line.

Jig A fishing *lure* that is jerked (or jigged) to appeal to fish.

Kelt A salmon or steelhead that has spawned recently.

Lateral line A visible line along the body of many fish, formed by a series of sensory pores.

Leader The length of line between the *mainline* and the hook, lure, or fly.

Lever drag A form of *drag* system on a reel, adjusted by moving a lever on the reel's side.

Lie A spot where a fish will hide, rest, or feed.

Livebait Any bait that is used live.

Loading/compressing the rod Putting a bend in a rod when casting, to give impetus for the *cast*.

Loop The shape formed in a fly line as it unfurls during the *forward* and the *back-casts*.

Lure An object attached to the end of the fishing line designed to entice fish.

Mainline The main fishing line on a reel.

Mending A way of creating less *drag* on the fly line after it lands on the water.

Monofilament Fishing line made from a single strand of nylon filament.

Neap tide The tide with the least difference between levels of high and low water, occurring during the first and last quarters of the moon.

Nymph The immature form of many insects.

Panfish Members of the Centrarchidae family; also a term for any small, edible freshwater fish.

Pectoral fins The front pair of fins on a fish, usually located on either side, behind the *gills*.

Pelagic Relating to the open ocean. Pelagic fish spend most of their lives in the upper ocean.

Playing Fighting a hooked fish to tire it out so that it can be brought to hand for unhooking.

Plug A fishing *lure*, usually designed to be *cast*.

Point fly The last fly in a team of flies, farthest from the main fly line.

Popper A surface *lure* with a concave face that splashes water, or "pops," when retrieved.

Presentation The art of casting the fly onto, or into, the water, and presenting it to the fish in the most natural way possible.

Reel seat The fixture that holds a reel in place on the fishing rod.

Retrieve To bring the fly, *lure*, or bait back to the angler after the *cast*, either by hand (fly-fishing) or by turning the reel handle (lure- and bait-fishing).

Rig The assembly of end gear, or *terminal tackle*.

Rise The act of a fish breaking the surface of the water to take an insect.

Run (1) A rapid movement away from an angler by a hooked fish. (2) A fast-flowing stretch of a river.

Running line The thin section of a fly line, lying behind the head section of a fly line.

Sandbank A usually submerged plateau or bank of sand that may be uncovered at low tide.

Setting the hook Securing the hook in the fish's mouth; also known as striking.

Sight-casting/sight-fishing Fishing for, or casting to, fish that you can see.

Sinking fly line A fly line made from material that sinks completely beneath the surface.

Sink-tip A floating fly line that has a sinking section at the end, varying in length.

Slack tide The brief period between the *ebb*

and the *flood tides*, when the current is weakest.

Smolt A young salmon ready to migrate to sea. By this stage it has the silvery color of an adult.

Snag (1) Rocky or foul ground that can trap lures, hooks, and weights. (2) To catch a hook, lure, or weight on an underwater obstruction.

Spawn (1) The eggs produced by fish. (2) The act of a fish producing or depositing eggs.

Spin To fish with *spinners* or *lures*.

Spinner A *lure* that revolves when retrieved; also a general term for a wide range of *lures*.

Spinning reel A reel with a nonrotating *spool*.

Spool The part of the reel around which the line is wound.

Sport fish A fish that is sought by anglers.

Spring tide The tide with the largest difference between high and low water, which occurs around the time of the new and full moon.

Strike/striking To sweep the rod back to secure the hook when a fish bites.

Stripping/strip retrieve To retrieve the fly line by using your hands to pull it in.

Stripping basket A perforated "basket" that attaches around the angler's waist, to store the excess fly line produced when *stripping*.

Swim Part of a river or lake fished by an angler.

Swim bladder The internal organ that enables a fish to control its buoyancy.

Tag/tag end A short section of redundant line that has been trimmed down after tying a knot.

Take The action of a fish taking a bait or hitting a *lure*.

Taper The part of the fly line that gradually decreases in diameter toward the hook.

Tapered leader A *leader* that tapers from thicker to thinner line, with the thinner end being attached to the fly or *lure*.

Terminal tackle Items such as hooks, *lures*, weights, and swivels that are attached to the end of the line; also known as the "end gear."

Tippet The thin, end section of the *leader* to which a fly is tied.

Trace Part of a *rig*, consisting of a line and hook that are attached together.

Troll To pull *lures* or *baits* behind a boat.

Vent The anus of a fish.

Waders Waterproof hip- or chest-length overalls, often incorporating boots.

Weight-forward (WF) fly line A fly line in which most of the weight is in the forward section of the line, making it easier to *cast*.

Wet fly A fly that fishes (sinks) below the surface.

Wet wading Wading without *waders*, usually in tropical waters, wearing appropriate footwear.

Wind knot A knot that can appear in the *leader* or *mainline* when casting, generally with *braid* or fly line, which weakens the line.

Resources

ORGANIZATIONS

Organizations and associations in North America that deal with fishing rules, techniques, and tournaments and other events.

American Carp Society
www.americancarpsociety.com

American Sportfishing Association
www.asafishing.org

Angler's Addiction
www.anglersaddiction.com

Canadian Sportfishing
www.canadian-sportfishing.com

Carp Anglers Group
www.carpanglersgroup.com

Crappie USA
www.crappieusa.com

Federation of Fly Fishers
www.fedflyfishers.org

Future Fisherman Foundation
www.futurefisherman.org

International Game Fish Association (IGFA)
www.igfa.org

International Women Fly Fishers
http://intlwomenflyfishers.org

National Ice Fishing Association
www.nationalicefishingassociation.org

Sportfishing Canada
www.sportfishingcanada.ca

Trout Unlimited
www.tu.org

Trout Unlimited Canada
www.tucanada.org

Walleye Central
www.walleyecentral.com

FISHING TRAVEL

Companies that offer advice or arrange fishing vacations:

American Fly Fishing Travel
www.americanflyfishingtravel.com

Canadian Fishing
www.canadian-fishing.ca

Gordon's Guide to Fishing Vacations
www.fishingvacations.com

Fishing International, Inc.
www.fishinginternational.com

Leisure Time Travel, Inc.
www.leisuretimetravel.com

Reel Women Fly Fishing Adventures
www.reel-women.com

World Wide Fishing Guide
www.worldwidefishing.com

FORUMS

Internet forums and information websites where anglers share tips and up-to-date catch reports:

Bass Pro Forums
http://forums.basspro.com

Fishing Talks
www.fishingtalks.com

Sport Fishing Forum
www.sportfishermen.com

World Sea Fishing
www.worldseafishing.com

MAGAZINES

North American magazines of interest to anglers.

Canadian Fly Fisher
www.canflyfish.com

Field & Stream
www.fieldandstream.com

North American Fisherman
www.fishingclub.com

Fly Rod and Reel
www.flyrodreel.com

American Angler/Fly Tyer
www.flyfishingmagazines.com

Saltwater Sportsman
www.saltwatersportsman.com

Sport Fishing
www.sportfishingmag.com

STATE AND PROVINCIAL INFORMATION

Government websites covering licensing, rules and regulations, fish species, and other state- or province-specific fishing information.

Alaska Department of Fish and Game Trip Planner
www.sf.adfg.state.ak.us/statewide/resource

Florida Fish and Wildlife Conservation Commission
http://myfwc.com

Hawaii Division of Aquatic Resources
www.hawaii.gov/dlnr/dar

Montana Fishing Guide
http://fwp.mt.gov/fishing/guide/default.aspx

New York Department of Environmental Conservation: Fishing
www.dec.ny.gov/outdoor/fishing.html

British Columbia Ministry of Environment Fish and Wildlife Branch
www.env.gov.bc.ca/fw

Ontario Ministry of Natural Resources: Let's Fish Ontario!
www.mnr.gov.on.ca/mnr/fishing

South Carolina Department of Natural Resources
www.dnr.sc.gov/fish.html

Angling safety

TRIP ITINERARY

• Always let others know where you are going and when you expect to return.
• If fishing in a remote area, leave your trip plan with a resort owner or dock operator.
• Write your trip plan on a piece of paper and stick it under the car windshield wiper.

WADING

• Wading can be treacherous in the spring, when the water is high or late in the fall, when the water is cold. Start wading in the shallows, so you can gauge the current and depth before venturing deeper. Wade diagonally rather than straight into the current.
• Rocky streams are slippery. Take small, slow steps, feeling for the bottom with one foot and supporting your weight with the other. Steel cleats or felt boot soles may help.
• A wading staff, tied to a wading belt, can be a handy aid in fast water.
• Always be aware of the tides changing and of rapidly rising water.

WATER SAFETY

• An ability to swim is essential to be safe near and in water; be sure that you always follow the BSA's Safe Swim Defense.
• Be aware of the correct first-aid procedures relating to near-drowning victims.
• Whenever you are in the water or afloat, remember to practice the buddy system.
• If you are wading in deeper water, or are in a boat or canoe, always wear an approved personal flotation device.
• Avoid alcohol, which is a factor in half of all drownings among teenagers and adults.

SAFETY AFLOAT

• Check the weather forecast before venturing offshore, and keep an eye out for gathering clouds—the signal to get onshore fast. A responsible angler should learn the water and carry an accurate depth map and compass.
• A serviceable boat-repair kit is essential for emergencies. Check running lights to ensure they work properly.
• Learn the boating laws of your state and those of the Coast Guard.
• A good flashlight or lantern is essential for signalling to oncoming motorboats.

MINOR INJURIES

• Take a first-aid kit to treat cuts, scrapes, sunburn, and insect bites. Take care when landing fish, preferably wearing gloves. Spiny fins and sharp teeth and gill covers, such as on walleye, can make nasty cuts that may get infected. Be especially wary of catfish spines. Use tweezers (sterilized) to remove slivers of fishbone from a wound.

HOOKS

• Always be aware of the path of your fishing rod and line when casting to prevent the hook or line from catching on something, such as another angler! If a wound does occur, never try to remove a hook that is near an artery or from the face or near an eye, or from any other sensitive area. If the barb is embedded, let a physician remove it—never try to remove an embedded hook by pulling it back the way it went in.

HYPOTHERMIA

• Dress appropriately for cold and wet weather. Wear a hat and the proper footwear, and carry rain gear to keep yourself and your clothing dry. Eat energy-boosting foods and drink plenty of fluids. Don't push yourself to a dangerous point of fatigue.

HEAT REACTIONS

• Protect yourself against heatstroke and heat exhaustion by staying well hydrated. Drink plenty of water; don't wait until you feel thirsty to drink or it may be too late. Wear a hat in hot weather, and use sunscreen to prevent burns to the skin.

Index

Acknowledgments

FOR DORLING KINDERSLEY

Senior Editor Richard Gilbert; **Senior Art Editors** Susan St. Louis, Gillian Andrews; **Production Editor** Jonathan Ward; **Managing Editor** Stephanie Farrow; **Managing Art Editor** Lee Griffiths; **Production Controller** Sophie Argyris; **Indexer** Chris Bernstein (this edition).

FOR SCHERMULY DESIGN CO.

Creative Director Hugh Schermuly; **Project Editor** Cathy Meeus; **Designer** Steve Woosnam-Savage; **Editors** Gill Eden, Jo Weeks; **Indexer** Lynn Bresler (original edition); **Illustrations** Andy Steer, Sally Pinhey, Colin Newman; **Commissioned photography** Mike Good, Gerard Brown.

PUBLISHER'S ACKNOWLEDGMENTS

Dorling Kindersley and **Schermuly Design Co.** would like to thank the following for their invaluable help with this book: Becky Alexander, John Bailey, Nick Helleur, Simon Peters, and Helen Schermuly. We would also like to thank all the manufacturers who generously supplied fishing tackle and equipment for photography: Delkim, Drennan, The Friendly Fisherman, Gardner Tackle, Hardy Greys, Korda, Masterline, Rok-Max, Sportfish, and Veals.

AUTHORS' ACKNOWLEDGMENTS

This book is for wife Islay, my two daughters, Isabel and Molly, and my sheepdog Jess. A special thanks goes to my parents and my two brothers. My thanks to Nick Hart, Graham Hill, James Warbrick-Smith, Pete McLeod of Aardvark McLeod, Gerhard Laubscher and the FlyCastaway guides, Del Thompson, Chris Woollven, Shaun Fenton, the people at Hardy & Greys Ltd., John Bailey, Steve McGuire, Tourism Ireland, Rodney Goodship, Miles Essex, Cato Bekkevold, Kristian Keskitalo, Eddie Read, Dave Box, Alastair Brew, Ed Truter, and Ricky Jacobs.

PICTURE CREDITS

The publisher would like to thank the following for their kind permission to reproduce their photographs:

(Key: a-above; b-below/bottom; c-centre; l-left; r-right; t-top)

Alamy Images: Reinhard Dirscherl 123t; Jeff Greenberg 11tr; Images&Stories 136tr; Jeff Morgan tourism and leisure 126tr; David Kleyn 116-117b; Wolfgang Pölzer 129t; Dave Porter 119b. Cathy Meeus: 73bl.
Henry Gilbey: 1b, 1t, 3-2, 5br, 6-7b, 8-9, 10b, 11b, 12b, 13t, 14bl, 14cra, 15, 16-17, 18b, 19tc, 19tr, 24c, 31br, 31cr, 36cra, 37br, 37tl, 39tr, 40, 43b, 43cb, 51b, 51cla, 54-55, 56, 57br, 57cla, 57cra, 57crb, 57tr, 58bl, 58clb, 58cra, 59b, 59cra, 59tr, 60bl, 60br, 60cl, 61b, 61cl, 61cr, 61tr, 62bl, 62br, 62c, 63bc, 63bl, 63br, 63t, 64ca, 65b, 65cra, 66cra, 67cra, 68-69, 74br, 75bl, 75cl, 75r, 76b, 77bl, 77br, 77tr, 78-79b, 79tl, 79tr, 82br, 83br, 83cr, 83t, 84bl, 85br, 85ca, 86bl, 87clb, 87t, 90-91, 92b, 92cra, 93bl, 93br, 93t, 94-95b, 95br, 95tl, 95tr, 96b, 97br, 97c, 97tr, 98br, 99bl, 99cra, 99t, 101br, 102bl, 103bl, 103br, 103cr, 103t, 104cra, 104crb, 105bl, 105br, 105t, 106bl, 106-107b, 107cr, 108b, 108cra, 109br, 109c, 110br, 111bl, 111br, 111t, 132b, 137b.

Brad Harris: 100br, 101t.
David Lewis: 80br, 81br, 81cl, 81t, 88crb, 89t, 89tc.
Brian O'Keefe: 67b, 112bc, 112-113b, 113tr, 121t.
Photolibrary: OSF / Doug Allan 138b; OSF / Keith Ringland 122b.
SeaPics.com: Mark Conlin 114-115.
Shimano: Shimano UK Ltd 5cla, 25br, 26bc, 26bl, 26br, 26cl, 27cl, 27cr, 47c, 76cra, 78cra, 80c, 82cra, 86cra, 88cra.
Richard Stewart: 126-127b;
Ole Wisler: 89bl, 89br.

All other images © Dorling Kindersley
For further information see: **www.dkimages.com**